2000

To Isab

8·28 2

Debbie

AMAZING GRACIE
A Dog's Tale

By Dan Dye and Mark Beckloff

Illustrations by Meg Cundiff

WORKMAN PUBLISHING • NEW YORK

Photographs on pp. 167–171, 176–7 © Tim Pott
Photographs on p. 174 (b) © Tatjana Alvegaard

Library of Congress Cataloging-in Publication Data

Dye, Dan.
Amazing Gracie: a dog's tale /
by Dan Dye, Mark Beckloff and Richard Simon.

p.   cm.

ISBN 0-7611-1937-X

1. Great Dane—Missouri—Kansas City—Biography. 2. Dye, Dan.
3. Beckloff, Mark. I. Beckloff, Mark. II. Title.
SF429.G7 D94   2000
636.73—dc21   00-040808

Workman books are available at special discounts
when purchased in bulk for premiums and sales promotions as well as
for fund-raising or educational use. Special editions or
book excerpts can also be created to specification.
For details, contact the Special Sales Director at the address below.

Workman Publishing Company, Inc.
708 Broadway
New York, NY 10003-9555
www.workman.com

Printed in the United States of America

First printing October 2000
10 9 8 7 6 5 4 3 2 1

For Gracie
and for every other
best dog in the world.

acknowledgments

This project most certainly would never have come to fruition without the vision and generous involvements of the following people:

Tanya McKinnon, our agent at Mary Evans Inc., who believed in us and this project from the moment we met. Her powerful agenting skills are surpassed only by her ability to overdeliver on everything she promises. We thank the gods (or was it the dogs?) for bringing her to us.

Richard Simon, friend and writer extraordinaire. Imagine 100 tons of writing talent compressed into one unassuming, funny, native New Yorker. His skillful wordsmithing kept improving this book all the way through. Working with Richard was a dream and his contribution to *Amazing Gracie* immeasurable.

Ruth Sullivan—truly a writer's editor. Ruth's intelligent editing and thoughtful wit made a Great Dane–sized difference in telling Gracie's story. Thanks, Ruth—you're the best. And warm pawshakes all around to our littermates at Workman Publishing—Rosie, Meghan, Elaine—for helping this project along its way, and especially Peter Workman for embracing Gracie's tale from the beginning.

contents

While Gracie's tale is true, some places, dates, events, and human names have been changed or combined to protect the lives and sensibilities of the innocent, and the not-so-innocent.

foreword

When an energetic eight-week-old albino Great Dane came into our lives one freezing January day, we didn't realize that our future business advisor and spiritual guide had arrived. She was deaf, and partially blind in one eye. She had a delicate constitution. But her tenacious and generous spirit would soon reshape our ideas, our careers, and our destinies. She would inspire us to believe in ourselves.

People know us best for our entrepreneurial success as the founders of Three Dog Bakery; what they don't know is that we owe it all to a gigantic deaf dog named Gracie. But even though Gracie sowed the seeds of our success, this isn't a book about "making it." This is the story of a dog who was born with the cards stacked against her, but whose passionate, joyful nature helped her turn what could have been a dog's life into a victory of the canine spirit—and, in the process, save two guys who thought they were saving her.

—Mark Beckloff and Dan Dye

One

Kansas City Blues

lue is a nice word for how I felt. I must have looked like a cliché of mourning: gray late-November Sunday afternoon, me in raggedy sweats and a two-day beard, slumped down in a Sears BarcaLounger that looked almost as good as it had the day I rescued it from a Dumpster my freshman year in college. All I needed was a half-empty bottle of whiskey, a crow on my shoulder, and an ashtray full of unfiltered cigarette stubs to finish the picture: MAN GRIEVING LOST LOVED ONE. It didn't make it any easier that the loved one was my childhood best friend of eighteen years—my dog, Blue. The phone could ring all day; I just sat and stared at it. I wasn't trying to avoid people. I just didn't have anything to say. Except to Blue. And she couldn't hear me anymore.

There aren't any diplomats or charm school graduates among my friends and family members, so their attempts to comfort me about Blue usually had the opposite effect. "She's probably happier now" was a favorite, along with "you can always get another one"—though nothing could top "thank God it was only a dog!" Only two people managed *not* to make me feel worse. One was Anne, my friend and fellow copywriter at Midwestern Company, who had lost her beloved golden retriever, Arthur, only a few months earlier. The other was Mark, my best friend, new housemate, future business partner, and generally the soul of good sense, skepticism, and bad taste.

Mark Beckloff and I had just gone in on a house together, a dilapidated "mansion" on Holmes Street in the heart of Kansas City. We planned to fix it up and sell it for a cool profit that would let us bankroll our business idea—as soon as we came up with one. For now it was our home until we did well enough to live somewhere else, or one of us pulled a *Double Indemnity* on the other—something I almost never considered. Blue's passing hadn't left us entirely dogless, because there were still Sarah and Dottie, aka "the girls," Mark's canine contribution to the household. He likes to think he's their human companion. Reality check: The girls are Mark's proud owners. Sarah's a two-year-old black Lab mix who's always in a good mood, especially when she's eating something Mark has to wear the next day. Dottie is an uncontrollable force of nature in the deceptive form of a year-old Dalmatian. Dottie wreaks havoc when she's in a *good* mood; only her spots keep people from mistaking her for a tornado.

Sarah, Dottie, Mark, and Anne gave me the most valuable gifts you can offer someone who's grieving: solitude and, occasionally, quiet company. Then one frigid morning a few weeks later, Anne added another great gift to quiet caring: distraction.

It was one of those bitter late-January days when you start wondering if a foot of snow might take the edge off the cold, and Anne, who always says her blood is too thin for Missouri winters, came into the office looking unseasonably happy. The fun-loving, energetic mom of two kids, Anne has the kind of call-'em-like-I-see-'em honesty that people associate with Harry S. Truman, who came from the same hometown. She's also a former prom queen with a way of flirting that always reminds me of a waitress in a greasy spoon—you know she doesn't mean it seriously, but it still makes you feel special. And once in a blue moon I get the eerie feeling she can read my mind.

I was a little suspicious about her good mood despite the single-digit temperature, and asked what was up. "Nothing!" she said brightly. How was her weekend? "Fine!" When I finally demanded to know what was going on, she pretended to be indignant: "Can't a gal be happy for no particular reason? Is there a law against being happy around here?" I knew better than to keep trying and went back to my work, which was just as well since we were up against a tight deadline on a new print-ad campaign for the Oh, So Delicioso! account.

They were expanding their "authentic sauces" line beyond "a bit o' Italy in every drop!" to "a bit o' Spain" and "a bit o' the Orient." Anne guessed that the company's authenticity experts must have logged grueling months of fieldwork in taco-terias and chop suey joints across the Midwest. (Market research had just told us that our leading contenders, "Oh-so es buen-o!" and "Ah, so—it's Oh-so!" didn't have the authentic foreign feel so prized by regular consumers of exotic canned goods.)

Anne left for lunch with a breezy "later, handsome!" but more than an hour later she wasn't back yet. I ran out to grab a slice at La Pizzateria Rusticana.

When I got back I found Anne crouched under her desk. I was just starting to think that the pressure of the Oh-So account had finally pushed her over the edge when she stood up, staggering under the weight of what looked like a small pony. She was beaming at the creature in her arms: a puppy. A squirmy and, for the moment, *little* Great Dane named Merlin.

He was a funny-looking guy, blue merle coated except for his cocoa brown eyes and the dark mask around his mouth that looked like a purple puppy version of Fred Flintstone's five o'clock shadow. His ears had just been cropped, and they were taped flat over his head with a bandage that reminded me of the bonnet on Whistler's mother. The way he was squirming around, you would have thought Anne had doused his fur with itching powder. Everything tickled him—if a puppy could laugh, Merlin had a case of the giggles. As it was Anne was doing enough giggling for the two of them, dropping barmaid lines like "baby, where ya been all my life?" in her husky alto. It was as if someone had taken my mature, wisecracking, accomplished colleague and replaced her with a wisecracking seven-year-old girl. If Merlin had been a man, I'd have worried about the spell he was casting on her, but it's hard to doubt the intentions of a puppy. Watching them, the Oh-So deadline vanished.

He wasn't even two months old and there wasn't much dog body to speak of yet, but he was bursting with puppy energy, all excited about being alive. As I cradled him in my arms, all the wonderful things I missed about Blue melded into one amazing and ineffable force I felt thrumping away in Merlin's heart—dog spirit. I wondered if I'd ever feel that force in my own life again.

Anne was transformed. Every day for the rest of the week she came in bubbling with stories and Polaroids of Merlin in action—getting a bath, wrestling with the dirty laundry, gnawing on his own tail, eating, sleeping, breathing . . . The temperature hadn't clawed its way above the twenty-degree mark in five days but Honolulu Annie hadn't even mentioned it, let alone taken personal offense the way she usually did. The reason was obviously Merlin. I could see how cute he was, and how much joy he gave her ("Yeah, yeah, yeah. Right in the middle of the rug. Adorable."), but by the end of the week I realized that I just wasn't sharing her joy. I was starting to narrow my eyes and grit my teeth whenever I saw her smiling. It was a subtle change, but she picked up on it.

"Something bothering you, hon?"

"Ha. Me, bothered? Never."

"You sure about that?"

"Yep."

"Maybe something you can't put into words?"

"Look," I snapped. "If something was going on in my subconscious, don't you think I'd know about it?"

"Hmm. Well, let me know if anything does bother you, okay?"

Not likely. I felt the way you do when your best friend falls in love, and suddenly the running buddy who gave you all that no-strings attention is focusing the spotlight on someone else—in this case, someone who generally has his face in a bowl of soggy kibble. Merlin was a walking reminder of everything about Blue that was gone. It seemed like everyone I knew had a dog, and they were all so darn happy about it. I couldn't even get away from it at home, since Mark had the girls, who might as well have been his shadows the way they stuck to his side. (Of course, *real* shadows don't shed, or beg for treats whenever you're cooking.) The girls were great in their way, especially if you have a soft spot for hyperactive narcissistic adolescent canine maniacs—which the historical record seems to suggest I do. And even though Sarah and Dottie hung out with me more and more, I could never shake the thought that they weren't Blue, and they weren't technically mine, even if we were living under the same leaky roof.

At the stroke of noon, my phone rang. "Listen, Dan, I hate to bother you . . ." It was Anne, calling from the other side of the office. ". . . but I have a problem, and I really need your help."

I turned halfway around to look at her, but kept talking into the phone. "What kind of problem?"

"Well," she said, with a serious look. "It's Merlin's sister. She needs our help!"

It sounded like a call from the Justice League. I tried to swivel all the way around but ended up dropping the phone on my foot. "Oww—Merlin has a *sister*?"

Five minutes later we were in my car.

two
Finding Grace

As we drove shivering to the breeder's house in my five-year-old, partially heated (driver's feet only) Hyundai, Anne told me that Merlin's sister was the last of the litter, and because she was deaf, no one wanted her. I don't know anything about Anne's family tree, but it wouldn't surprise me to learn that she had missionaries swinging from every branch. Her eyes burned with the fiery zeal of the righteous, and I felt like the heathen locked in her sights.

Picturing a Great Dane breeder I half-expected to see a rambling and weather-beaten old farmhouse, maybe with a barn ingeniously converted into a state-of-the-art kennel, all the furnishings in (what else?) Dane-ish Modern. One of the farmhands—Clem—would eye us suspiciously until we mentioned dogs, and then his leathery skin would soften with a warm smile as he asked if we'd come "to speak a whelp from the last litter" then send us "up the road a piece to see the old man"—Zeb. All right, maybe I watched too many episodes of *Lassie* when I was a kid. So I was surprised to crunch up a long gravel driveway and pull up in front of a tiny 1950s ranch-style tract house. As I put the car in park, I could see that the attached garage had been turned into some kind of rec room, and the garage door replaced with sliding glass patio doors.

I turned off the engine and tried to make sense of the strange picture in front of us. Hanging inside the patio doors were pieces of fabric that ended in tatters three or four feet from the floor, as if hungry sharks had shredded defenseless curtains in a feeding frenzy and would soon be coming back for more. I'm not sure what expression was on my face (probably the one I save in case an elevator cable snaps), but I'm certain that Anne was studiously ignoring it. As we got closer to the house I realized that the grime on the glass doors was actually a million slimy nose and pawprints, which covered the glass like a camera lens smeared with butter to shoot the close-ups of an aging star.

Anne motioned to the doors. "Don't be shy—have a look!"

Peering inside, I could make out a herd of very large animals in various states of repose around what looked like Ozzie and Harriet's living room on bad acid. I was about to ask Anne where the dogs were kept when I realized—these *were* the dogs!

I'd always known that Great Danes were big, but in the same way I knew it about dinosaurs—I'd never actually seen a grown one in person. These were the biggest canines I had ever seen, and there seemed to be *dozens* of them! Great Danes the size of small cows sat up quickly on couches and chairs. I wouldn't have been entirely surprised to see one of them set down his pipe while another peered at us over a pair of reading glasses. When they saw us, some twelve angry hellions kneed and elbowed each other to get closer, crashing against the glass. A couple of them propped themselves upright, standing more than seven feet tall on their hind legs, looking *down* at me and howling for flesh. I thought of those amazing aquariums where you can go almost nose to nose with a creature that could be Jaws's delinquent nephew while some smart-aleck tour guide announces, "Just think—all that stands between you and three thousand pounds of prehistoric death drive is a flimsy little piece of glass!"

A deafening roar arose from behind the glass. The word *barking* does as much justice to the sound they made as *crunching* does to the noise of a jackhammer. If you haven't spent time around this giant breed, the first time can be a frightening experience. I expressed my fear with a three-foot backward jump—right into Anne.

Luckily, that flimsy glass was tempered against even the kamikaze attempts of raging Great Danes. As I helped Anne to her feet, she batted her eyelashes and said, "I like a man of action."

"Yeah, well," I said, brushing the gravel off my jacket, "if you meet one, say hi for me." She responded with a succinct punch to my shoulder, walked to the front door of the house, and rang the bell. I walked backward. If the glass doors *didn't* hold, I wanted to see 'em coming.

The door was opened not by Clem or Zeb but by a short, squat man named Al, who grunted and let us in. With his sleeveless undershirt and unlit cigar, he could have been Danny DeVito's uncouth older brother—not exactly what I was expecting. The other thing I wasn't expecting was the smell.

Imagine walking into a solid wall made of all the foulest odors you've ever smelled. Let it ferment for about thirty years and you'll have a mild sense of the stench that occupied Al's house and pressed the walls outward. I could tell that Anne wasn't exactly enjoying the experience either, but she was having a good old time watching *me.* My eyes teared, my nostrils burned, and my inner ear seemed to think I had been launched into weightless orbit around the earth.

After quick introductions and small talk about Merlin (Al's side of the conversation consisted mostly of nodding and the occasional "yup"), the breeder extended us a grumbling invitation to have a look at the creature he called "the little mistake." When Al opened the door to the rumpus room the dogs exploded in our direction like a multiple-warhead missile. I could tell now that they were less intent on devouring us than on bathing us, sniffing us, and then reporting the results. After about a minute of slobbery pandemonium I noticed Al pointing at something and trying to shout over the noise. He was saying either "Dasher threw up and a goner" or "That's her—the runt in the corner."

There, in the farthest corner of the room, all by herself, was the loneliest little dog I ever saw: a snowball of white and gray fur in that rolling sea of black-patched harlequins. Anne had never told me that this puppy was albino to boot. Merlin's sister was lying on the bare cement floor facing the wall, oblivious to the mayhem surrounding her. The other Danes seemed to sense that something wasn't quite right with her. Maybe it was her color, her floppy uncropped ears, the way she didn't respond to the sounds they heard bubbling around them—but they left her alone. All of them—even her own mother. All she had for company was a dirty, gnawed-up tennis shoe and the threadbare terry-cloth belt from an old bathrobe.

A dog big enough to bear a saddle mistook Anne's pocketbook for a chew toy, and while Anne tried to reason with him I knelt down next to Merlin's little sister till we were almost eye to eye. It was a face I would never forget. She looked at me with huge blue eyes (think Paul Newman or a cloudless sky on a summer day, only bluer), the right one rimmed in black as if she'd gone just a bit overboard with the eye liner. Like most Great Dane pups she hadn't begun growing into her skin yet, and it hung on her tiny frame like an oversized velvety jumpsuit. Her ears hung down like the flaps on an old aviator's cap, making her whole head look heavy with the burden of sad secrets. She raised her eyebrows as if to ask, *Can I tell my story to you?* Then she barked—a short, quick bark, not loud at all but deep, like it was coming from way down.

"That's a new one." Al was still standing in the doorway. "Never heard her make a peep before. Dumb albinos."

She seemed startled by my close presence, but she got to her feet like a clumsy young foal and sniffed me. When I smiled, her short little tail went up like an antenna and started wagging, though she stayed a couple of inches away. The second I began petting her, though, she came right up and started licking my face, my hand . . . every part of me she could reach. Just as I was wondering if anyone—human or canine—had shown her any affection at all in her short, lonely life, she did something unique in my experience of dogs. She raised her forehead to mine and very deliberately nuzzled my nose. Then she stepped back, looked into my eyes, came forward, and did it again.

I don't claim to be Dr. Dolittle, but I felt I could hear in my heart what she couldn't put into words. *You know I'm the one. Now stop fooling around and get me outta here!*

Anne had just wrestled back her pocketbook, and chose this moment to tell me that the puppy was scheduled to be put to sleep the next day. She didn't say another word; just gave me her own version of sad-puppy-dog eyes. As if she still needed to convince me. I scooped up my new friend from the cold floor and held her in my arms. Anne smiled a sweet smile of victory. If she *was* a missionary, there wouldn't be an indigenous religion left in the world.

I thought Al would be happy to see the little gal get a home, but it didn't look that way. "She'll be a lotta trouble, y'know," he warned us. "You're probably not doing her a favor. I mean, it's no kind of life." He gave us some brochures about caring for Great Danes almost as an afterthought, and we sprinted back to my frozen Hyundai. I was happy to leave Al, his hounds, and their collective aromas far behind.

I told Anne that I would hold the dog so she could drive and at least warm her feet, and she was happy to accept. When we'd settled in I looked over at her and saw not a victory smile, but the same goofy seven-year-old-kid grin she was wearing the day she got Merlin. It still looked goofy to me, but as I turned back to Merlin's sister I felt the corners of my own mouth turn up in an unfamiliar (and possibly goofy) way of their own. My fuzzy pal looked up at me, sniffed me with the power of an industrial vacuum cleaner, and wiggled from nose to butt until she found just the right spot in my lap. This time the message was loud and clear: *I knew you were the one, too.*

three

Here Comes Trouble

The sun lit up the inside of my mobile deep-freeze unit. Anne drove as I held the towel-swaddled bundle in my lap. Instinctively seeking heat, the puppy rolled around to press her nose against my belly. I could feel the car and my heart filling up with the warmth of dog soul. Until I got a twinge of guilt. What about Blue?

I don't gamble, but I like to think that if I did, my James Bond–like ability to conceal my thoughts and feelings would soon have me puffing a Havana in a Monte Carlo casino. I'd have a moniker that reflected my cool demeanor and my rivals' grudging respect: "Cool Hand Dan," or maybe "The Silent Americano."

Anne reached over and gave my blanketed bundle a rub. "Thinking about Blue, hon?"

My Monte Carlo career went up in smoke.

"All right," I said. "Yes. I feel guilty. She only died eight weeks ago yesterday and I just—" Anne was giving me such a strange look that I stopped in midsentence. "What? What's the matter?"

"Eight weeks ago."

"Yeah," I said, a little impatiently. "Eight weeks ago yesterday."

That strange look again. "Dan, Merlin and his sister were born eight weeks ago."

Dawn was rising slowly over my brain. "So that means . . ."

She squeezed my arm. "The week Blue passed away."

"I, uh . . ." For some reason my throat got tight. I'd had a pang of worry that my taking Little Miss Nosy home was somehow betraying Blue, or her memory. Now I felt like this was a sign from Blue, her way of letting me know that she didn't want me to be alone. That is, without a dog in my life.

Anne touched my arm.

The puppy, completely unmoved by our conversation, had fallen asleep in my lap.

Anne smiled. "Hey, who knows? Maybe she's a blessing."

I looked down at the round-bellied baby dog. "Maybe." I sure hoped so.

Back at my place I whisked Merlin's sister past a napping Sarah and Dottie and put her in the big back bedroom where all my prized personal possessions (Matchbox cars, comic books, beer can collection) were still safely boxed and stacked away. I set her up with bowls of food and water, plenty of paper on the floor, and a big old blanket in the opposite corner. I felt bad about locking her in, but the old door wouldn't close unless it was locked, and I couldn't give her the run of the house because of what Sarah and Dottie might do to her, especially before they'd been properly introduced. Seeing me about to leave, she raised her head and furrowed her brow: *Are you leaving me already?*

I reassured her with a bunch of kisses, which she seemed to take as proof of my honorable intentions. To keep her company I plugged in a radio tuned to a mellow-music station, locked the door, and hightailed it back to the office. Anne and I were halfway back before I remembered that the puppy probably wasn't a fan of *any* music, let alone "Soft Sounds to Cushion the Hard Knocks," as the deejay promised. But I wasn't worried about leaving her there. A tiny dog in a room full of sealed boxes—what trouble could she possibly get into?

I rushed through the rest of my workday and flew out of the office at 5:59. A few blocks from home two police cars sped past me on the road. I didn't give it much thought until I pulled up to the house and saw the patrol cars in my driveway. I raced up the front steps, heart pounding. I couldn't imagine what was happening, but the girls were going berserk and it sounded like Mark and a dozen other guys were yelling at top volume. A couple of our neighbors were huddled on the sidewalk, no doubt discussing how the neighborhood had gone down the tubes since we'd moved in.

Inside, things looked as bad as they sounded. Despite the bitter cold outside, Mark was as flushed and sweaty as if he'd just run a marathon. He was struggling to hold the howling Sarah and Dottie back from the stairs and at the same time shouting at the policemen on the second floor, who couldn't hear him. They were busy yelling things like, "Just take it easy and open the door very slowly," and, "You don't want to make us open that door!" It had the unmistakable ring of *NYPD Blue*, but it looked way too real.

I had to call Mark's name three times before he registered that I was there. "What the hell's going on?"

"Somebody broke into the house!" he yelled back. "I must have walked in on him! He locked himself in the back bedroom and now he's tearing it apart! I called 911—" The dogs kept lunging forward, trying to get out of Mark's grip. "*No*, Sarah! *No*, Dottie!"

I clenched my teeth. It couldn't have been hard to break into the house. If I described the place as "ramshackle," I'd be letting you think it was in better shape than it really was. We'd been there only three weeks when we found out the roof was not what experienced homeowners call "rain resistant." Still, with all the house's faults, I couldn't believe someone had broken in. I shouted to Mark, "Are you kidding me?" He was starting to answer when we heard the crash of falling boxes.

"See?" Mark yelled. I saw, but I wished I couldn't. Some maniac was in the house, locked in a room with all my prize possessions and destroying the place. Then it hit me—my puppy was in there, too! What if he hurt her? My God, what if he killed her? I had to protect her.

"Listen up," one of the policemen was yelling. "You got five seconds to come out with your hands over your head, or we're coming in, door or no door!" I could hear two of the other officers—one of them either a woman or a really high tenor—barking into walkie-talkies, and for a second I wondered if they were talking to each other, even though they couldn't have been three feet apart in the hallway. Maybe it was some strange police regulation we civilians wouldn't understand, but they could have talked to each other till doomsday for all I cared.

"The dog!" I grabbed Mark's shoulder. "What about the dog?"

Mark's left hand was holding Sarah's collar and his right hand was holding Dottie's. "Fine!" he yelled. "They were barking their heads off when I got in, so they—"

"No, no," I yelled, pointing frantically toward the stairs. "*My* dog!"

A mysterious series of thoughts flashed across Mark's face—we'll never know what they were. He must have settled on one like, *Dog? Dan doesn't have a dog anymore. Okay, he's losing it. I'll just keep him calm until the proper authorities arrive . . .* He gave me the most condescending look I'd seen since the nuns in Sunday school. Nodding sadly with one eyebrow raised, he said, "Listen, Dan, why don't you go for a walk or something, since—"

I cut him off. "Mark," I yelled louder. "I have a dog! A *new* one. A puppy. She's upstairs. In the back bedroom. With all my stuff!" Mark looked even more baffled than before. "I was gonna tell you. I just got her this afternoon at lunch. She's deaf. She's—"

Before I could finish explaining that she was a pedigreed descendant of champions regardless of her disability and, by the way, one of the cutest dogs who ever lived, Mark shot past me and flew up the stairs yelling, "Wait! Wait!" Sarah and Dottie did a synchronized double take from Mark, to me, to Mark, then flew after him. Mark was shouting, "Don't break the—" when I heard a loud long *crrrr-AAACCCK!* that was the unmistakable sound of a heavy boot kicking through a brittle antique door. There was a second of silence followed by an explosion of laughter, which I chased up the stairs two at a time.

Framed by the shattered doorway to the back bedroom was the strangest sight I'd ever seen, not counting the costumed reenactment of the Missouri Compromise at last year's Fourth of July

RiverFest. In the center of a completely trashed room, surrounded by Sarah, Dottie, Mark, a policewoman, and three policemen holstering their guns, was my unnamed, unarmed little puppy—more to the point, her snow white rear end. Her little rump was up in the air, wiggling with a glee seconded by her tail, and she was making small snarling noises that could only have intimidated something smaller than, well, an eight-week-old puppy. She was totally impervious to the sharp barks of disapproval coming from Sarah and Dottie and the expletives from the boys in blue.

As I stepped past the remnants of the door she stopped moving for a moment, and her little snout shot straight up like a periscope. She sniffed, spun around in my direction, then with a flourish rose up to her full height (about ten inches), tossing back the blanket she'd been burrowing under. I don't know if she achieved the effect she was aiming for, because the blanket was still draped over one eye, making her look a bit like Veronica Lake. That is, if Miss Lake had fuzzy cheeks and a penchant for chewing on fine leather shoes—in this case, half of the only pair of dress shoes I'd ever owned. I shook my head mournfully. "Not my imitation Ballys!"

The vibrations of the door getting ripped from its hinges hadn't budged her attention away from her sole-searching activities, but something—I'm guessing my familiar smell—turned her around. She glanced at the crowd assembled around her, and if she was startled by her audience she didn't show it. When she spotted me her tail started wagging double time, and she trotted up and deposited the remains of my right shoe at my feet. She gazed up at me, panting a little at the effort of subduing the wild loafer, and I realized that she was offering me the spoils of her kill.

While Mark apologized to the officers and I tried to explain about her deafness and apologize for every bad thing that had happened since the oil embargo of 1973, the policewoman, a freckle-faced redhead, knelt down next to the proud little hunter. Out of the corner of my eye I saw her scratch under Shoe-Killer's chin, a gesture accepted with the dignity of a small empress. "Well, well," said Officer Kenner, picking up Her Imperial Majesty and looking her straight in the eye. "Ain't we just little Miss Grace-Under-Pressure?" The subject of this compliment couldn't hear the praise any more than she heard the chaos she'd just provoked. Still, she must have sensed the good feeling behind the words. She turned around and said thanks the only way she knew how. She tried to lick the officer's freckles off.

Kenner smiled up at me. "What's her name?"

"Uh . . ." I felt guilty of puppy negligence. In the hectic few hours since I brought Miss Grace-Under-Pressure home, I hadn't given a thought to naming her. Then inspiration struck. "You know, you almost guessed it," I said, covering smoothly. Gesturing to everyone—canine and otherwise—in the room, I announced, "Sarah, Dottie, officers . . . meet Grace Dane." For her part, Gracie furrowed her white brow as if to acknowledge the significance of the moment, then craned her neck around and gave me the lightest nip on the chin. As my eyes met her baby blues, it was clear that the nip had multiple meanings: *Can't you get rid of these pesky intruders? When do we eat dinner around here? And where's the other shoe?*

OF FEAR AND FUR

Now, you'd think that all this was really more than enough action for one day, or one year. You'd think that we didn't need any more traumatic incidents before bedtime. And you'd be right. Unfortunately, no one was asking you at the time, which is how we discovered that the house might, on top of everything else, be haunted.

After the police left, Mark took Sarah and Dottie for a predinner promenade and I let Gracie wander around, acclimating herself to her new digs at her own pace. It was my turn to cook, so I made a light dinner of pasta (in open defiance of my starving fat cells, which were screaming for a greasy cheeseburger), covered Mark's bowl, and settled down on the couch in front of the TV. To keep our electric bill low, we were scrupulous about keeping the lights on only in the room we were in; for the living room, that meant the very dim glow cast by my beloved Elvis lamp—a ceramic sculpture of The King in Vegas whites, undaunted by the brass tube running through the top of his pompadoured head. Suddenly I heard a sound that went through my bones. I held my fork in midair. *Again!* It was a sound that made my marrow cringe, the low moaning and scraping sounds you'd make if your nails were goring grooves into a blackboard. I tried to raise a thought from below the well of fear that filled my head, but nothing came up. Then the noise—again!

Maybe we had it coming. Maybe we should have *anticipated* a ghost. I don't know. A few months earlier, when the two of us had pooled all our meager resources to make a down payment on this massive, hundred-year-old, ten-bedroom mansion, ghosts were not a priority; keeping it from collapsing was. All we knew about its history was that for many years it had served as a home for mentally disabled boys. One of our smart-aleck friends said if we bought the place, we'd be carrying on the tradition of housing "troubled" young men. Actually, before we bought the house, we wondered if it might harbor a ghost or two. All right, *I* wondered. I figured that in a hundred years someone *must* have died here. My twisted mind conjured up images of afflicted boys, beaten and half-starved by their sadistic keepers, roaming the moonlit corridors in straitjackets and moaning helplessly through dislocated jawbones at their plight. Now I should probably say right here that we never heard anything to even vaguely suggest that such scenes had occurred, but that's not really the point. The fact is, a lot of my extracurricular knowledge comes from the weekly regimen of horror movies I took in between the ages of nine and twelve—one part of my education I've never let go to waste. I hadn't mentioned the ghost boys to Mark because . . . well, because he's too literal-minded to fathom things that fall outside the realm of scientific description. Now I wished I'd told him, but it was too late. Too late . . .

Again! The noise was growing louder, coming closer. What was it? At that moment I knew, as if I'd known it all my life. It was the hungry ghosts of the starved and shackled boys, lurching down the hallway like a platoon of Frankenstein monsters, coming slowly but inescapably for the one thing that could slake the aching hunger in their tortured souls—the taste of human flesh!

Right when I thought I'd explode if I spent another second sitting motionless on the couch, the sound subsided, and suddenly the house was eerily quiet. Then the scraping, scruffing noise came again . . . this time even closer—so close, in fact, that it sounded like it was coming from the other side of the wall. Just as the violent pounding in my chest threatened to crack open my rib cage, I turned and saw the source of the noise: There, in the dark and echoing corridor, was little Gracie—humming to herself, shuffling her oversized paws along the hardwood floors, and loudly sniffing every square inch of the place.

Naturally, I was pretty relieved to discover that it was not a ghostly horde of junior Freddie Krugers, but only my puppy investigating her new home. It turned out that Gracie had never learned to pick up her feet when she walked because she'd never been taught. When the other pups in the litter were being tutored in doggy basics, little Gracie was ignored, left to make her own way. As a result, she just shuffled along—but thanks to her spirit, she always shuffled with grace. Just how much grace she had already had in her short life, I was about to find out.

four
Little Miracle

The next morning I brought Gracie to see Dr. Benjamin, a veterinarian who Anne had told me was the foremost Great Dane expert in the area. I wondered if there were dozens.

If Hollywood ever moved James Herriot's dog stories from the Yorkshire countryside to the American heartland, the boys at Central Casting would sell their mothers to get Dr. Benjamin for the part. His salt-and-pepper hair, lined, ruddy face, and tired but bright eyes were the textbook features of the Kindly Old Veterinarian. When he saw Gracie a warm flicker of recognition swept across his face.

"Ahh, it's little Miracle! How are you, sweetheart? It's nice to see you!" He leaned down to let her kiss him and showed us into the examining room.

Gracie's tail flapped like a turbo-charged metronome. She obviously thought it was nice to see him, too, but I was baffled.

How did he know her? And why was he calling her "little Miracle"?

Dr. Benjamin examined Gracie while he talked, and she submitted to it like it was a game. "When this young lady was just a few weeks old," the ol' doc began, anticipating my question, "a family came to choose a pup from the new litter." He shone a light into her ears. "Now, as I heard it from the breeder, their young daughter went straight for your Gracie, picked her up, tripped, and fell square on top of her!" Gracie gave a woof of agreement—a deep, throaty woof midway between Greta Garbo and Marlene Dietrich. "Well, that little girl cried so loud that no one looked to see if *you* were hurt, did they?" Since he was holding Gracie's mouth open and peering down her throat, I don't think he expected much of an answer. "It wasn't until late the next day that the breeder noticed her belly was swollen and her breathing was short and fast. When he brought her in, I found two broken ribs." He stared into her eyes. "Aren't you a brave little one?"

"Is that how she got her name?" I asked.

Dr. Benjamin laughed. "No, poor thing." He scratched her under the jaw. "That was just a warm-up!"

Dr. Benjamin explained that he'd taped Gracie's ribs, and she grew so fast that she was fine in just over a week. Then a few days later the breeder brought her back to have her ears cropped, trimmed to stand in two razor-sharp upright points. (Some people say a dog with drop [floppy] ears is more likely to get ear infections or break blood vessels in the tips of the ears, but I don't buy it—would you chop off your toes to make sure you never stubbed them?) Personally I consider cropping as desirable as foot binding, but I did wonder why Gracie hadn't been cropped when Merlin had.

"I already had a suspicion she might be deaf, but breeders can be a little . . . calculating when it comes to deaf pups. Since she was only here for a cropping, I decided not to test her hearing unless the breeder asked me to." He picked up her tail and checked out her rump. "I gave Gracie her anesthesia and suddenly, before the surgery even began, she died."

"She *died?*"

He nodded. "She was dead for several minutes. Probably a reaction to the anesthesia, but we never found out for sure."

"How . . . ?"

"Oh, I never gave up on her," he smiled. "I tried everything to bring her back, every resuscitation technique in the book shy of opening her up and massaging her heart. After a minute with no response, my nurse thought I was crazy. After two minutes, I started to wonder myself, but for some reason I just couldn't stop pressing her heart, blowing in her little mouth, waiting. There wasn't a single vital sign registering, but I was convinced that somewhere inside there was still a spark of life, and I couldn't quit trying until the spark caught. Another minute, two—it felt like hours, but I kept going. My nurse was *begging* me to stop. And then those big eyes flickered—once, then again, then they stayed open and the monitors jumped back to life like they'd never even stopped for a second! Never," his voice caught, "never in my career—and I've practiced veterinary medicine since before you were born—have I seen such a thing."

Dr. Benjamin took off his glasses and wiped them with a tissue. When he put them back on I could see that his eyes were moist, but he was smiling, a warm smile that lit up his cascades of little wrinkles. "From that day on she's been Miracle to me."

"Well," I said, "I guess she is a little miracle. But you made it possible."

Dr. Benjamin shook his head vehemently. "Oh, no. No, no, no. I don't do miracles. I just try to do my best each day, and keep my eyes open to the miracles happening around me. That day I didn't have to look very hard." He leaned over Gracie. "Not very hard at all."

I was silent. Gracie got up on her back legs, put her white paws on his chest, and lightly butted her nose against his. If she felt like throwing her affections around, I could let it go this once.

That night I lay in bed thinking about Gracie and her name. *Grace.* The night before, inspired by Officer Kenner's remark, I had named Gracie a little ironically—charmed by her sweet clumsiness. Twenty-four hours later I felt as if she'd already earned her name twice. In the grace that brought her back to life— I guess that's obvious. But also in the grace with which she'd arrived in my empty life. As I stared at the ceiling I had a strong feeling that this goofy pup nuzzling into my armpit was going to give me a few things I hadn't known I was missing. Grace is everywhere, all around us. As Dr. Benjamin said, I would just have to do my best, and keep my eyes open to see it. The year ahead was going to give me plenty of chances.

five

Smell the Flowers

ife in a house that hasn't been renovated since the repeal of Prohibition has a few quirks. One of them has to do with windows three feet wide and twelve feet high. Since the wood frames are always shrinking or swelling, and glass isn't the greatest insulator, big old windows do little to keep out the cold or even the cutting winds; on the other hand, they let in a flood of sunshine, whether you want it or not. This leaves you with two options: shelling out the bucks for a castle's worth of drapes ("Give me something that doesn't let much light through, maybe black or *off* black. Do you sell it by the acre?") or learning to love sunshine. Guess which we chose.

Just as my alarm clock crowed to greet the dawn, I jumped at the soft, wet, velvety tongue lapping my neck. Too small to climb down from the big bed on her own (and, at only eight weeks, already too much of a lady to soil the sheets), little Gracie stood over my eyes, flapping her tail with cheerful impatience. I wasn't embracing the new day as cheerfully as she was.

Now, I like to consider myself a generous person. I was a Boy Scout, I saved hurt birds, I walked old ladies across the street and didn't wait to be thanked. So I didn't mind that my newfound companion wasn't doing her version of Oliver-Twist-rescued-from-the-workhouse: waking up early to wax the floors and make my pancakes. What I did mind was that I still had to get up and travel across the tundra to a soul-killing job, be confined for nine hours fighting a deadline that hadn't gone away just because Gracie showed up. I had work to do, a mortgage to pay, a life to get. And I wasn't feeling grateful for it.

"I can't spend the day playing," I said out loud. "You get that, don't you?" I tilted my head toward her for emphasis. She licked my nose.

I lowered her to the floor (which she promptly moistened), washed and dressed quickly, and led her to the stairs. She ran ahead of me to the edge of the top step, dipped her paw off the edge twice as if she were testing the water, and turned back to me expectantly: *I can do this, can't I?* She didn't show even a hint of fear—but ran, tested, turned around, and waited for instructions. I guessed she was big enough to navigate the steps one at a time, but not now. I wanted to carry her down just this once. We were going for our first walk. Or so I thought.

Despite my years of canine experience, I'd never actually taken a dog on her *first* walk before. It turned out to be a greater challenge than I'd expected. Much as we tell ourselves that dogs are creatures of instinct, there are certain things they're unequivocally not born knowing. For example, it turns out that dogs are not born with a keen understanding of the concept of "collar" or "leash," let alone "go for a walk." As Gracie proved very quickly.

For some reason, instead of collaring her in the kitchen where there were limited possibilities for escape, I let her out into the snow-blanketed yard, following with the little collar and leash Sarah and Dottie had long since outgrown. When she began capering around the yard instead of instinctively submitting to the collar (and the man holding it), I made my next brilliant move: I started yelling. "Gracie! C'mere, girl! C'mere Gracie! Com—"

I stopped myself in midword and looked around to see if there were any witnesses to the bleary-eyed dope calling a deaf puppy. None, thank God. So I capped it all off with a move that guaranteed failure: I chased her.

It's not that Great Dane puppies are particularly fast, or that Gracie was a particularly speedy Dane pup. It's just that when a puppy gets to go wild in a big yard for the first time in her whole two months of life, the last thing she's inclined to do is calmly walk up and present her neck for shackling. Come to think of it, there probably isn't a creature on earth that gravitates toward collaring, but let's just say Gracie was less inclined than most.

In a movie the chase would have lasted less than a minute; by then you'd have the idea of what the dumb guy was going through. Since this was real life, and Gracie had no intention of bowing to cinematic conventions or anything else, it lasted close to half an hour, Gracie happily letting herself be cornered and then darting out of my grasp as I lumbered panting after her, and ended only when I plopped down on the back porch, exhausted and defeated. That's when Gracie decided to trot over to me, cuddle up to my leg, and cock her head: *Don't you wanna play anymore?*

What a dope I'd been. She wasn't running away from me—she was playing! And all I had to do was step off the playing field to see it. I stroked her little round head, laughing at myself. Then I reached over and put the collar on her neck without her making so much as a peep. She was curious about it, scratching and pulling for maybe ten whole seconds, then completely lost interest. Until I attached the leash.

With the first click of the clip to her collar's D-ring, Gracie blasted off into outer space. Or would have, if not for the leash. This time I wasn't planning on letting go, though she did everything her pint-size body could to change that, tugging at her chain with futile desperation. Despite her diminutive size, she was jerking my body six ways to Sunday. Maybe this was how it felt to rope a bucking bronco, or how it *would* feel if the bronc were roughly the size of a teddy bear.

I drew her close and knelt down, stroking her and telling her not to worry, and finally she seemed less afraid of the leash than curious. We were ready to hit the road. Or at least I was.

As soon as we walked out the gate Gracie bounded outward from the house with the joy of someone who had obviously never had a day job. For all I knew she'd never experienced sunshine directly before, and it agreed with her. She ran down the path ahead of me, then bounced as the leash stretched out to its full length and recoiled back, confused. Despite her armed truce with the leash minutes before, she couldn't seem to understand why an invisible force field was keeping her from roaming freely through the world. Then she forgot again and bounded outward once more, only to bounce back again.

While Gracie kept practicing her own version of horizontal bungee jumping, I tried to guide her gently up the block and back again as fast as possible. At the same time my brain was spinning "Oh, So Delicioso!" slogans with growing desperation ("It's the Most-O!" "High and Low-So!" "Put It on Your Roast-O!") My strides moved ahead of her or behind her as she yo-yoed around, running up and bouncing back. Since I had never raised a dog from a pup before (Blue had practically raised me), all I could think of was getting Gracie's first walk over with so she'd be used to it later, when she knew which bodily functions to save for the occasion. But she had other ideas.

"C'mon, girl!" I said, with a yank on the leash. "Com—" Then once again remembering her hearing loss, I lowered my voice to a whisper. That way no one could *prove* I'd been talking to a deaf dog.

"Look," I said, "it's just—" I stopped myself again and then knelt down close to her in the snow, petting the back of her neck to get her attention. When she caught my eye I shifted to telepathy. *That way,* I telepathed, nodding my head toward the end of the block for emphasis. *There, good. Here, bad.* Then, as if that wouldn't be clear to anybody, I picked her up, walked a few steps, and put her down again without breaking pace.

Later Mark and I would teach her our own version of ACSL—American Canine Sign Language. We came up with a couple of basic hand gestures to start with. *Sit* was arms fully extended with palms flat out. *Chowtime* was pointing to my open mouth, followed by the signal for *come.*

Come was her favorite. I would throw my arms out wide and wiggle my fingers. When she came to me I always rewarded her with lots of love and hugs, even if she'd done something wrong. I never tricked her with that gesture to get her to come close for a scolding. It was a very special gesture that meant only one thing: Come and get some love. But all this would come later; today we were just trying to go for a walk without dislocating my shoulder.

She scampered along beside me, seven quick steps for one of mine (that's twenty-eight in dog steps—counting every leg). Just as I started to think I might get back in time to make something to bring for my lunch, she planted her feet again, her white forehead wrinkled with an earnest curiosity that I'd never seen on human babies, let alone canine ones.

You wouldn't think a 12-pound puppy could stop a 175-pound man dead in his tracks, especially while he was being propelled forward by the momentum of his advertising genius, but there it was. Gracie had stopped short, nosing under the snow at something hidden at the edge of the sidewalk. Flowers. She pounced on them, sniffed them, almost embraced them with her nose, and wouldn't budge. I kissed my economical brown-bag lunch good-bye.

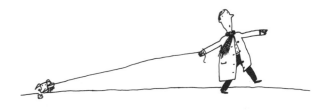

Flowers? Here? Now? What kind of flower has the audacity to grow in a Kansas City winter? It was a tiny cluster of blue wildflowers, maybe two inches high, popping up under the snow against all logic. All I wanted to do was walk the dog without getting fired, and here she was trying to stop and smell the . . .

I stood under the clear cold sky, marveling at Gracie's refined sense of smell (Hubbell telescope to my magnifying glass), as she explored the delicate complexities of what looked to me like a flowering weed. My whole life, she was showing me, was a series of fears and desires, goads and goals. I wanted to get away from poverty and into prosperity, away from someone else's business and into my own, away from meaningless existence and into—I tried not to think about it.

And Gracie was telling me, *forcing* me, to stop and smell the flowers. To see and taste and feel the beauty that was there for the asking, all around me, for free. Two days before I'd been the saddest slob on either side of the Mississippi. Now I was a boy with his dog on a beautiful sunny day, snow on the ground and not a cloud in the sky. The world could wait a few minutes. We had flowers to smell.

❀

six

Sister Trouble

In the turmoil of bringing Gracie into the household, it never occurred to me that Sarah and Dottie might actually have *feelings* about Gracie, let alone that those feelings might be hostile! After all, Dottie and Sarah were merely awkward teens, while Gracie was an adorable baby pup; their coats were dark or spotted, whereas Gracie's was (mostly) white as snow; they had typical brown dog eyes, and Gracie's eyes were bluer than—okay, maybe I was showing the slightest bit of favoritism. And even though Mark could never be accused of preferring anyone to Sarah and Dottie, it was only natural that he was curious about the newest member of the household, too. But Sarah and Dottie had *definite* feelings about Gracie's intrusion into their lives, feelings that the girls weren't exactly subtle about expressing. Then again, maybe they knew that subtlety wasn't the best vehicle for making a point to the youngest member of the family.

Gracie hadn't known a friend in the world until the afternoon I met her, and now she thought she had a house full of them. She was happy enough to have me and Mark around, but she was clearly overjoyed that there were two other creatures in the family *who looked like her!* Not that anyone was going to mistake the three dogs for triplets, or even for the same breed; but if you suddenly found yourself with two other humans on a planet full of bug-eyed monsters, you probably wouldn't sweat the fact that your fellow humans had different skin color, clothing tastes, or politics from yours. When Gracie came into the kitchen and it really sank in that Sarah and Dottie shared *all* her important qualities (four legs, paws, tail, snout, droopy ears, fur), she ran to greet them with the doggy body-language equivalent of *Hey girls, what's shakin'?*

If dogs have their own secret Masonic handshake, nobody had shown it to Gracie, because Sarah and Dottie responded, in chorus, with the canine version of *Back off, punk, if you value your life!* It wasn't just that they were barking louder than we'd ever heard them; they were also doing things dogs usually do only in books or movies, like baring their fangs and snapping their jaws. Picture the two hungriest crocodiles in a moat, and all of it directed at little Gracie!

Mark practically leaped across the kitchen table to grab them by their collars. I scooped Gracie up and turned my back to Sarah and Dottie, staring at them over my shoulder while they kept auditioning for the remake of *Cujo.* Mark was holding them back, but their sudden snap from sweet to vicious scared *me.* Gracie reacted in the only way appropriate for a puppy in her situation: She started hyperventilating.

"I don't believe it," Mark was saying. "I've never seen them like this. This is insane!" As if to make Mark's point, Dottie tried to lunge in my direction.

But Mark has never been a pushover for animals, unlike—well, unlike somebody else you might have read about in these pages. He's the nicest guy in the world to any creature he runs across, but the second one of them crosses the line Mark doesn't wait an instant to let it know who's the alpha dog; that creature had better get in line *now!* Which accounts for the sonic boom that shook the floorboards and actually drowned out the two juvenile delinquents. "Sarah, Dottie—SIT!"

The terrible twosome froze on their paws like they had just gone for a Sunday stroll on Mount Sinai and found themselves face to face with the Big Guy. "*SIT!*" They exchanged a worried look of *Uh-oh—we messed up big time!* before their guilty rumps sank trembling to the floor. "DOWN!" As they lowered their torsos to the tile, I swear I heard them sniffling. Was it fear? Remorse? A sudden understanding of the implications of their actions? Probably not; they were just scared of getting yelled at. But at least Mark's booming voice had cowed them into momentary submission, even if it was at the expense of my hearing.

Gracie was still triple-panting in my arms, so I turned around to show her that the scary monsters of a moment before were now quivering chickens. As I turned I half-formed the thought, *Maybe this isn't such a good*—but there was no stopping the momentum. As soon as Sarah and Dottie saw Gracie's puffing little snout they almost exploded out from under Mark, barking, *Get the intruder! Intruder alert! Get the intruder!* or barks to that effect.

Mark somehow barked them down again, and once they were safely (for the moment) at his feet he said, "Dan. Why don't you take Gracie upstairs for the evening? I think we'll all feel better if she has a change of altitude." His eyes were bulging a little, and he was speaking with the kind of calm I imagine the captain of the *Titanic* had to draw on ("Folks, it looks like we won't be taking our regular route to New York . . ."), so I figured this wasn't the best time to debate strategies. I took Gracie upstairs and tucked her into bed with me. I was so worried about her I decided to forgo a repeat of *L.A. Law* and read until bedtime. After all, tomorrow would surely be a brighter day.

The next morning, knowing that Sarah and Dottie were still warming Mark's feet, I managed to sneak downstairs, Gracie in my arms, without waking them. The morning had begun innocently enough, with our now-standard adventures in how *not* to collar and leash your new puppy and a wonderfully leisurely walk, but when we got back to the kitchen door Sarah and Dottie were waiting for us like Rizzo and Frenchy from the tough-girl gang in *Grease*. I'd like to say that two not-yet-full-grown female dogs didn't intimidate me, but this is nonfiction, so I'm constrained to telling you what actually happened. After waiting a few minutes for them to lose interest (*Ah, he don't got the nerve to come back in the house with that little half pint, right, Riz? You said it, Frenchy—he's down to two legs already, and he better keep his distance if he wants to keep what he's got*), I decided to run the gauntlet.

Tucking Gracie into my jacket, I backed into the kitchen to keep my body between hers and theirs. Gracie must have forgotten her terror of the night before, though, because she squirmed out of my jacket and slid down my leg to the floor before I could stop her.

Have you ever been to a dog race? You know that little electric rabbit the dogs chase around the track? Well, the absence of a twitchy nose and pointy ears on Gracie didn't seem to give Sarah and Dottie a moment's pause—they went stampeding after her from the kitchen into the living room with me stumbling after them, calling, "No! Stop! Wait!"

I might as well have been cracking a whip and yelling, "Mush!" Gracie scampered underneath the coffee table with Dottie close behind. Too close, as a matter of fact—since Dottie was twice Gracie's height, instead of scooting under the table, she skidded into it like a Mack truck on an icy road, flipping the table on its back and shattering my treasured Elvis lamp into a million slivers.

Scared that they'd cut themselves on the sharp Elvis edges that carpeted a patch of the floor, I ran over to form a human shield between dogs and shards. This might have worked if Sarah hadn't been headed in the same direction from a different angle. There's a law of physics that explains why we weren't able to occupy the same space at the same time, but no one had ever explained it to Sarah: She tumbled into the small tower of magazines and newspapers I'd been meaning to tie up for recycling, pitching it over in a slow-motion avalanche of newsprint and glossy pages and sprawling on top of it in a four-legged split. I ended up on all fours as well, my body arched in a position that must exist in very advanced yoga, with deadly bits of Elvis glinting up at me. As I raised my head I found myself staring into Sarah's slightly dazed eyes. I didn't have time to savor the moment, because Dottie was already up and yowping after Gracie, who seemed, from the corner of my eye, to be bouncing around the room like a renegade superball.

Naturally, this galvanized Sarah, but her efforts to get to her feet met with about as much success as you'd expect from a newborn foal on roller skates; her scrambling sent her plowing into my neck, snout-first. As I toppled to my side I grabbed Sarah with both hands, landing her (not quite intentionally) on my chest in a position that would have made for a classic Hollywood kiss if Hollywood weren't so prejudiced against love between the species. Just as I was realizing that I miraculously hadn't landed on any ceramic fragments, Sarah sprang off me to rejoin the chase, which from the sounds of the destruction had already made a lap around the kitchen and back.

I gingerly got to my feet and yelled a few more commands from the "Wait! Stop!" category, knowing they'd have no effect on Gracie but thinking it'd be nice if *someone* listened. Someone did, only it was Mark, whom we heard before we saw.

"SIT! NOW!" From above, the thundering Biblical voice that would have struck fear into the hearts of pagans was restoring order to chaos. Well, semi-order. Sarah and Dottie stopped in their tracks while Gracie kept boinging around the living room.

"STAY!" I turned around and saw not Charlton Heston coming down the stairs but Mark, dripping wet, shivering in a bathrobe and wearing an expression that could scare the Phantom of the Opera. I didn't move (on the off chance that he was talking to me), and Sarah and Dottie didn't budge either. Gracie, however, was still going full tilt, and when she skittered into Mark the combination of her speed, his surprise, and his wet feet sent him sprawling with a very unbiblical "whoa!"

His sudden dethronement snapped Sarah and Dottie out of their obedient trance, and they tore after Gracie again, leaping over Mark like he was a log and Gracie the fox they were chasing. Seeing Mark temporarily in the beta-dog position boosted my own confidence. I followed the pack toward the kitchen, jumping over Mark myself and yelling a totally useless, "*Graceeee!*"

I found them in a standoff: Gracie cowering under a little stool stacked high with empty pizza boxes, Sarah and Dottie circling the stool and howling the canine war dance. I dove for Gracie, knocking over the stool and the Tower of Pizza, and rolled onto my back, hugging her trembling little frame close to mine. I was feeling heroic until I blinked and saw that we were now both at the mercy of our snarling captors. I was trying to remember how to do the second part of the fight-or-flight thing when suddenly a pair of much bigger furry legs stood directly in front of me.

"SIT! DOWN! STAY!" Mark had recovered from being body-checked by a creature shorter than his knee and was now back in charge.

He dropped to one knee between Sarah and Dottie, held them down by the scruffs of their necks, and bared his own fangs. "All right, ladies," he growled. "That is the *last* time you pull a stunt like that on your little sister. Gracie is here to stay, and you're gonna learn to live with it." They were whimpering like kids who see a spanking on the horizon. But they weren't facing a spanking;

they were facing something far worse, something most dogs can't even bear to contemplate. They were facing . . . TIME OUT!

Mark rose to a crouch, still clutching Sarah and Dottie by their scruffs. "I think what you two need is a little time alone." They both upped the whimpering to second gear, as if they knew exactly what he'd said, and the whimpers shifted to something like moans as he walked them toward the stairs. But did I feel for them? Ha! Well, yeah, I guess I did for a second, but I turned my attention to poor Gracie, expecting to see all the classic symptoms of Post-Traumatic Canine Stress Disorder. What I saw instead was Gracie staring up at me, with an expression of pure puppy pleasure. She nipped my chin, turned her tail to me, and, with a quick wicked look over her shoulder, dove under the nearest pile of boxes and started tunneling around. The little minx wasn't terrorized—she thought this was some elaborate game we were playing for her benefit, just like the leash-and-collar routine: *Hey everybody, let's all run around the house and make a great big mess!* As I got down on my knees to coax her out, I heard Mark's voice over my shoulder.

"Aw, did you lose your squeaky pork chop?"

"Very funny," I said, my hand latching onto Gracie's warm little tummy. "Especially from the man whose attack dogs are terrorizing my little bundle of . . . pandemonium." I scooped Gracie up and lay on my back among the boxes, holding her in the air over me. What a little clown.

"*Were* terrorizing," said Mark, dusting off his hands. "I don't think they'll be bothering the little furball here again. Ever." He headed for the coffee machine. In the distance I could hear the dim sound of dogs being horribly tortured—or at least locked in separate rooms without anything or anyone to play with for ten whole minutes!

"Beckloff's back," I said in my best movie-theater coming-attractions voice. "And this time it's personal!"

In the same time-honored spirit, Mark snarled, "Don't push me, man. I'm a coiled spring."

"Ooh, I'm shakin'!" I got to my feet with Gracie tucked under one arm like a loaf of bread—a very squirmy loaf. He forgot that I was protected by Ultra-Gracie—part puppy, part killing machine. I held her out toward Mark. "Kill, Gracie! Kill! Go for the jugular!"

Using a technique known only to bionic dogs, she slurped the side of his neck so thoroughly that he turned around to kiss her on the nose. He told her she had nothing to worry about from "those two sob sisters," and she seemed to believe him.

I wasn't so sure.

I put Gracie into one of the other empty rooms for the day, hoping that when Mark let Sarah and Dottie out, they wouldn't figure out a way to burrow through walls. I doubled the newspaper on the floor and left Gracie with a bowl of water, more food to nibble, and her two new toys, Mr. Right and Mr. Left (formerly known as

Dan's Dress Shoes). I felt awful leaving her for a whole day, so I tossed her a pair of sneakers to keep her company and, thinking *What the hell,* a wool sweater my aunt had given me last Christmas. Then I hightailed it to work, telling myself *Ten minutes late isn't really late,* but knowing I'd be lucky to get there by 9:30.

The moment I walked in the door that evening Sarah and Dottie were there to greet me, but without their usual enthusiasm—kind of an *Oh. It's just you.* I didn't know if the new attitude was because they'd been chastened by their time in the hole and blamed me for their punishment, or if they were feeling fresh guilt for having just torn Gracie limb from—

I ran up the stairs and swung open the door, only to be met by a surprising lack of disaster. The hallway light roused Gracie from what I assume was Zen meditation. I apologized for leaving her alone, and she forgave me with a ceremonial face washing, which continued while I cleaned up the floor and gathered the day's kill (two sneakers and a sweater that never even heard her coming). Then I picked her up and tiptoed out into the hall.

"Sarah? Dottie?" I whispered their names, figuring that if they were going to ambush me, they might at least do it when I was ready.

"Hey, come on down!" Mark had come home and was channel-surfing on the couch, a dog on either side of his feet. They were both so still they could have been practicing to replace those lions you see guarding the steps of museums and libraries. But as we came around the couch, Sarah and Dottie both snapped their heads in our direction and started to stand.

"Did I tell you to move?" Mark didn't move his eyes from the TV and spoke as calmly as he would to a baby.

Sure enough, Sarah and Dottie did a simultaneous "Eyes front!" as their butts dropped back to the floor in one fluid, synchronized movement.

Mark hit the mute button on the remote, "Okay," he said. "I've got it all figured out."

You may recall my mentioning that Mark's a very logical guy. He takes a scientific approach to everything—sees a problem from all angles, takes it apart, puts it together again, et cetera. Basically, all the things I couldn't do if you sat me in a room with a Fisher-Price toy, five steps of instructions, and a year to make it work. Not only can't I follow instructions, but other people's explanations end up sounding to me like grown-up talk in a *Peanuts* cartoon. So while

Mark was going on at length about what he'd done to get Sarah and Dottie in line, and what I should do to help drive the message home, I kept watching his hand move to emphasize his words. More to the point, I kept watching *Gracie* watch Mark's hand move, and try to catch it in her mouth each time it waved anywhere in her direction. And Mark just kept talking: "Mwah-mwah-mwah, mwah-mwah, mwah-MWAH-mwah-mwah . . ." Listening to his lecture made me wonder if deafness might actually have some advantages.

Eventually he seemed satisfied that his message of canine subordination had been understood, and he wandered off to the kitchen, leaving the four of us—me, Gracie, and the Piranha Sisters—alone in the room again. I could feel my heart slamming against my ribs; the term *shark-infested waters* came to mind. With the girls' eyes boring into Gracie and me, I was starting to back out of the room when I heard a voice bellow from the kitchen.

"Don't forget what I toldja!"

I leaned my mouth against Gracie's warm head and murmured, "I don't suppose you caught it, huh?" Gracie tilted up to face me, shining those baby blues and showing me just a hint of a smile.

Fortunately Mark likes to repeat himself. "Can't let 'em know you're scared. Gotta show 'em who's boss. Just sit down like you own the place."

I edged over to the couch, holding Gracie just a little tighter. Sarah's and Dottie's eyes never left us. I stepped over Dottie to the command center—Mark's spot on the middle cushion—and plopped down. I was trying very hard to act like I owned the place, but even forgetting the mortgage it was tough, especially with Sarah and Dottie giving me the hairy eyeball. I pretended to watch Peter Jennings talk about something that was clearly very important, Gracie seemed to be comfortably nestled in my lap and equally captivated by Peter's easy mastery of the world's events, and Sarah and Dottie had let their eyes drift back to the screen when the unthinkable happened: Gracie squirmed out of my arms like a greased piglet, slid off the couch, and plopped down on the floor directly between Sarah and Dottie.

I held my breath. Gracie shuffled her butt so she was in the same position as the girls, and looked from one to the other, panting eagerly, her tongue hanging slightly out of her mouth, no trace of fear: *Hey guys, did I get it right? Is this how you watch TV? Huh?*

Both dogs looked down at Gracie, then at each other. Sarah turned away and leaned over to lick her forepaw: *Oh, what's this? A speck of dust on my otherwise-pristine coat? We can't have that.* Dottie met Sarah's eyes, looked down at Gracie again, and shook her head, making a noise somewhere between a sigh and a snort: *Well, there goes the neighborhood.* Then all three of them turned to watch TV.

Sitting on the couch in the drafty living room, the four of us illuminated only by the flickering screen, it hit me that Mark was right: Gracie wasn't in physical danger from Sarah and Dottie. What neither of us knew was that now she was in *emotional* danger. Nature was playing a cruel trick—replicating a high school girls' clique right there in our living room.

Luckily, though, nature likes a balance and was about to provide the solution our puny human brains couldn't dream up: It's a lot easier to intimidate a creature half your size than one twice as big and growing.

Growing is an understatement for what Gracie was doing— it was more like *blowing up*, like when you magnify a picture to ten times its original size. She was twelve pounds when I got her at eight weeks old. Two weeks later she was more than twenty pounds. In another month she was almost forty pounds, and by the time her six-month birthday rolled around she already weighed eighty-five pounds! A doggy sweater that fit her on Tuesday squeezed the breath out of her on Thursday. If you watched closely, you could *see* her getting bigger. I got used to the look of polite terror in neighbors' eyes as they noticed paws the size of clown shoes and remarked, "Whoa! She's gonna be a *big* girl, ain't she?" They saw her galomphing along the sidewalk, stopping to play with the tiniest bug as though it was her equal in size and status, or toppling over as her hind feet got ahead of her front feet. Several people were rude enough to smirk when they found out her name was Grace; a few guffawed.

But no one was more stunned by Gracie's growth than Sarah and Dottie. You could almost see it in their eyes . . . their disbelief and anxiety at her ballooning stature. I would notice them looking at her and then looking at each other like they were wondering *Will she* ever *stop growing?* By five months she was their equal in size and weight. Grudgingly they began showing her a bit more respect, or at least wariness. But not affection. Still, I was determined to "mainstream" Gracie with them, even if it meant pain and heartache for a while. This was probably what Rudolph's parents were thinking when they sent him off to reindeer school.

The first thing Mark and I noticed once all three of the girls were in the same weight class was that Gracie worshiped Dottie. She literally followed Dottie everywhere, and tried her best to do anything she saw Dottie doing—if possible, at the same time. This included bodily functions; if Gracie didn't have any more to give when Dottie was still donating, she would make believe. About the only thing she *didn't* do was take a Magic Marker and draw dots all over herself. Now, most of us can't stand being mimicked for more than a minute or so, but if it bothered Dottie, she never let on—of course, that would have meant acknowledging Gracie's existence.

Although the whole relationship was baffling to me, Mark felt that it made perfect sense. We discovered this difference of opinion one night while we were tearing down the rotting plaster on one of the bedroom walls, the girls dancing around in the chips and plaster dust.

"It's obvious," Mark said, for no apparent reason. "She sees Dottie as an admirable female role model, and she wants to be just like her."

"How? Eat everything in sight? Run fast? Terrorize defenseless puppies?" I slammed the sledgehammer into the plaster, grunting. I made a serious dent in the wall.

Mark swung even harder, leaving what looked like a giant's punch mark, and turned to shoot me an *excuse-me?* look. "Are you insulting my dog? You're not insulting my dog, are you? 'Cause it sounded like you were insulting my dog."

"Listen, Jake LaMotta, I'm not insulting your dog. I'm just asking you to tell me what Gracie could possibly hope to learn from Dottie. Aside from how to pee."

Mark shook his head. "Okay, fine." He ticked off traits on his fingers: "Character. Determination. Loyalty. Courage." He searched for a word. "Grace under pressure." A smile flickered across his face. "You know—all the things she can't learn from you."

"Watch it, pal. I got a sledgehammer in my hands." I demonstrated my threat by leaving another dimple in the plaster.

Mark countered with a blow that went through the plaster to the wire netting behind it. Sarah and Dottie reacted like it was a snowstorm, leaping in the air like furry corkscrews to catch the debris. "Yeah. I'm about as scared of your hammer as I am of your killer guard dog over there." I looked around and saw Gracie off in the corner, wrestling with a dropcloth that clearly posed a lethal threat to her.

I paused to take a break from all the exertion, even if it was mostly Mark's. "Look. All I'm saying is I don't see what she thinks she's learning from Dottie that she couldn't learn from any other dog in the world. Like Sarah, for example."

Mark set his sledgehammer down and leaned on it, with the easy familiarity you expect of someone who's had experience on a chain gang. He looked at Gracie, then at Dottie, then Sarah, and Dottie again. "Spots."

"What?"

"Spots. That's gotta be it. She wants to have spots, so she figures if she acts like Dottie, she'll get some."

I sucked my teeth halfway out of my gums. "I see. Okay. Well. Thank you, Dr. Science."

Unfortunately all the emulation in the world wasn't going to make Dottie give Gracie the time of day, let alone spots, and it certainly didn't win Gracie any points with Sarah. Having first threatened to make lunch of their youngest sibling, Dottie and

Sarah had switched to ignoring her utterly. They nudged Gracie out of the way if Mark was talking to her, abandoned any toy they had if Gracie noticed and wanted to play, and actually ran away from her in the yard if she came over to where they were hanging out.

At first I couldn't believe what I was seeing. In my thinking about canine psychology, I always had the idea that whatever else dogs may do, however they might act out their inner feelings, one thing was for certain: Dogs are *never* catty. Well, Sarah and Dottie disabused me of that idea very quickly. They somehow managed to be incredibly catty while treating poor Gracie like a dog.

It was like watching the worst parts of childhood in an endless loop, knowing there was nothing I could do to explain to Gracie what was going on: *Look, sweetie, don't pay attention to those mean girls—they're just insecure, and they think making you feel bad will make them feel good.* Even if she could hear me, and even if she could understand my words, it probably wouldn't help any more than it had when my parents said the same kind of things to me.

All I wanted was to see her, just once, stand up for herself and put those two bullies in their place. But when the fateful day finally came, the only one of us who wasn't surprised was Gracie.

Within a week or so of Gracie's arrival the three girls had established a routine for breakfast and dinner that never varied: Each would get her own bowl, Sarah's and Dottie's on the floor, Gracie's up on a chair. Sarah would scarf up her meal in one or two deep breaths and trot off, leaving a few bonus crumbs for Dottie. Dottie took a bit longer to devour her own meal, then she'd slurp up Sarah's leavings before ambling after her. But Gracie's eating style was all her own. First she would give thanks: Before she even got near her food she'd look up at me, wag her tail, and lick her chops. Now, you might think this was just anticipation, but she did it at exactly this point before every meal—and never while the food was being prepared, when all the good smells were filling the air. Only after I'd been properly thanked would she move on to the complex process of eating, experiencing one kibble at a time (two if she was feeling ravenous) for a leisurely half hour to forty-five minutes before nosing around the house to find out where the action had gone.

One night when Gracie was a little over a year old, the routine got thrown. I still don't know why; maybe the moon was full, maybe Mercury was in retrograde, maybe I accidentally gave Sarah seven fewer kibbles than usual. For whatever reason, Sarah cleaned her plate. Now you might think Dottie wouldn't notice something like that, but only if you didn't know Dottie. She flipped Sarah's bowl over to see if Sarah had hidden the bonus kibbles as some kind of sick practical joke, then started jerking her head around frantically: *No! No! This can't be happening to me. It's all some horrible dream!* But this was no nightmare, my friend; it was all too horribly true—Sarah had not left Dottie a single morsel!

A different dog, possibly one with fewer spots, might have let it go; just shrugged all four shoulders and thought, *C'est la vie,* or *Que sera sera,* or a similar cliché in another language I don't speak. But not Dottie. After recovering her equilibrium, she coolly assessed the situation and trotted over to Gracie's area, where she began to sniff at the few kibbles Gracie had let fall to the floor. Big mistake.

Despite Gracie's fastidious eating style, a few kibbles always fell to the floor in the course of her meal (Great Dane jaws aren't exactly surgical tweezers). I assumed she didn't notice, because she never bothered to go after those stray bites; after all, she rarely finished what was in her bowl. But that night, between bites in her evening eat-a-thon, she sensed Dottie's unusual presence. Dottie had no sooner leaned down to put her mouth to the sacrificed kibbles than Gracie let out a roar and snapped her jaw with the force of a bear trap, right next to Dottie's snout—an inch closer would have taken off her sister's nose. Dottie reeled back in horror, and I grabbed Gracie by the collar as she snapped and barked, sending Dottie fleeing into the back of the house in a terrified blur of spots and whimpers.

Then without so much as a moment's pause, or even a glance at the scattered kibbles that she had just so ferociously defended, Gracie returned to her meal, finished it, and loped off happily to find out what Dottie was up to.

Dottie was still Gracie's idol—that never changed. But that night Gracie had drawn a line in the sand that neither Dottie nor Sarah ever tried to cross again. Basically she had told them, *Look, gals. You can pull all the snotty stunts you want, trying to make me feel like third dog out, but never* ever *mess with a gal's kibble. Get me?*

I was thrilled. My girl had finally stood up for herself. But then I found myself wondering, *Is this as good as it gets? Will they never show her more than grudging respect? Will it always be*

the demonic duo plus one, or will these three ever be a sister act? The next few months would answer all my questions, but not before a summer at the park that tried my faith in canine-kind.

Summer arrived in Kansas City with all its beauty, greenery, and lack of air-conditioning. Even if we'd been able to afford air conditioners for the house—an *if* the size of Montana—we didn't have the funds to run them. Instead we had to decide between opening the windows the six inches that our supermarket screens could cover and swinging them open wide only to be devoured by mosquitoes. Our solution? Spend most of our free time in the park with the dogs.

Naturally, it didn't occur to us that the wide-open spaces of the park would give Sarah and Dottie even more opportunities to torture Gracie socially. Then again, they probably didn't plan it that way—chalk it up to devilish inspiration.

Remember Monkey in the Middle, the game seemingly designed to let two older kids torture a little one without getting into trouble? (If you're a youngest child, I *know* you remember it.) Believe it or not, dogs have their version of this game, which I realized one Saturday in July when Mark and I brought all three dogs to the park. Dottie would get Gracie's attention then run off to make Gracie chase her; then she'd outrun Gracie and circle back around to where Sarah was, and Sarah would do the same darn thing. Gracie, the perennial good sport, played along, but after a while she was pooped and frustrated—like a kid who's invited to play tag and then told she's permanent "it." She came loping back to me, her long tail between her legs as if she was ashamed at having been fooled, while her wicked stepsisters joined their crowd, who were roaming around, swapping stories, and sniffing each other.

I was trying to mainstream Gracie, but I couldn't stand by and watch Sarah and Dottie ostracize her, so I decided to be another dog with her. If she ran to the other side of the park, I ran to the other side of the park; if she ran to the bench where Mark was sitting and reading or just soaking up rays, so did I. We jumped and spun in the air, we rolled over and over in the grass, we wrestled . . . After about ten minutes I was ready for a two-hour nap and Gracie was just getting warmed up. She stood panting expectantly with the look I knew so well by now: *What's the matter? Don't you wanna play?* I wanted to, but I couldn't. Who knew that being a dog was such hard work?

Soaking wet, I plopped down on the bench next to Mark. "Don't sweat it," he said without opening his eyes. "Not everybody has what it takes to be a dog." I shook my head at the indignity of it all.

In the distance I could see Gracie getting rebuffed by Sarah and Dottie once more. Then she noticed a new dog who was standing off to the side by himself—just like Gracie to befriend the wallflower. It was a linebacker of a dog, very thick and solid looking, kind of like—no, it *was* a rottweiler.

There are two schools of thought about rottweilers: Love

and Fear. The problem is, they're very territorial dogs without a strong sense of play once they're grown up, so depending on how they're raised, they tend to mistake a lot of things (hugging, dancing, moving) for hostility. I try never to generalize about dogs by their breed (unless it's to generalize about their good qualities), but I have to admit that the reputation of good rotties gone bad has always put me on my guard in their company.

Gracie was doing her *Hey, c'mon, let's play!* dance in front of this particularly large specimen—maybe 150 pounds of muscle and fang. At first he just watched her curiously, but then he started to shake his head in a strange way, looking somehow restless, even agitated. Just as the word *bearbaiting* popped into my head, Mark said, "Hey, isn't that a rottweiler? I don't know about playing with a rottweiler . . ." and we both stood up at the same time and shouted, "Gracie! Gracie!" Then we looked at each other and started yelling "Sarah! Dottie!" Obviously Gracie wasn't going to come to our call, but she might if she saw Sarah and Dottie running our way.

The girls stopped what they were doing with their crowd and turned toward us, but they didn't come. *Bad moment for you guys to be ornery,* I thought, and I took off toward Gracie. The rottweiler's hair was on end and he had lowered his head like an angry rhino about to charge. I kept yelling for Sarah and Dottie, and I heard Mark right behind me doing the same thing. But I felt helpless—the rottie could put Gracie in a world of hurt before we ever got there. I was puzzling over why Sarah and Dottie wouldn't come even to Mark's call when the strangest thing happened: They disappeared from their play group and materialized on either side of Gracie, snarling at the rottweiler in a way that made their first night with Gracie seem like a warm-up. Sarah pawed the ground in a convincing impression of a mad bull, and Dottie snarled and snapped like a . . . well, like a rottweiler. Gracie looked from side to side. Not to be outdone, she started barking, too—though it sounded suspiciously like her happy bark. I think she had no idea she was even in trouble!

The rottweiler, I'm happy to say, *knew* he was in trouble. I doubt I'll ever have the chance to see a rottweiler slink away in fear again, but this occasion will stick with me forever. Mark and I stopped where we stood, stunned by the minor miracle we'd just witnessed.

"Wow." Mark shook his head. "What can I say? Sisters are doin' it for themselves." He cupped his hands to his mouth and yelled. "Sarah! Dottie!" He took a deep breath. "GRA-CEEEE!" Naturally, they all came running.

Watching them charge toward us, I understood that while

Sarah and Dottie might snub Gracie, they saw her as part of their *gang* just the same, and anyone who wanted to hassle Gracie would have to go through them first—not a gauntlet any sane dog would want to run. They pulled up short at our feet, panting and woofing, all eager to tell about their adventure. As we walked back to the truck, I shook my head, awed by how subtle and complex relationships can be, and by the strange ways love can surface in the most unlikely circumstances. But more than anything I realized that I will never, as long as I live, understand dames.

seven

First Love

omething was wrong. Something wasn't the way it was supposed to be. I'd been feeling it for a while, but I couldn't put my finger on it until one November night when Gracie was walking me and pointing out the stars with her now-considerable nose. I still hated working in an office, still had a driving desire to be my own boss and for me and Mark to come up with that great idea that would free us from our day jobs, et cetera. But something was very wrong: Life wasn't as bleak as it used to be. Even I had to notice that I didn't feel quite so empty anymore, and the reason was a certain sniffing, snorting teenage dog who seemed to think I was all right. On the other hand, maybe I shouldn't have been so flattered, because Gracie soon showed that she wasn't *that* discriminating. I was about to find out that her heart had an open door.

When Mark and I first moved into our house there was a low wooden fence between our yard and the neighbor's. If we wanted to let the girls hang out in the yard (and we did—even when there were only two of them), we had to put up some kind of fence. Unfortunately the most economical kind was the least attractive good old schoolyard chain link. (Personally, I always thought something with wrought-iron spikes on top would have gone better with a house built in the style known as Early Addams Family, but as usual poverty outvoted taste.) We thought that ugliness was the only downside, but we soon realized there was another: our next-door neighbor, Mrs. McGuire.

We didn't even know there *was* a Mrs. McGuire in the picture-pretty Victorian house until the fence was halfway up, and by then it was too late. She was a retired English teacher whose children had long since grown up and moved away; her husband had died many years before, and her only real company was a feisty little Boston terrier named Byron. Byron rarely made public appearances; that is, Mrs. McGuire had him on a schedule that coincidentally never overlapped with Sarah's and Dottie's outdoor time. So we had very little proof that either of them existed. Until the fence went up.

It was a Saturday morning maybe three weeks after we moved in. The fencing guys were digging holes and pouring concrete, the girls were barking their approval, I had a headache, the phone rang, and I picked it up just as I was politely asking Sarah and Dottie, "*Will you please be quiet?*"

Then I realized I had just yelled into the phone. "Oh, I'm

sorry, I was talking to the dogs."

There was a dignified pause, followed by a slightly wavery voice. "Well, I certainly hope so. This is Mrs. McGuire, your next-door neighbor. With whom do I have the pleasure of speaking?"

Well, she had the pleasure of speaking with me, but the pleasure didn't last long once she confirmed that we were, in fact, having a fence put up, and that it was, indeed, chain link. It wasn't a hostile conversation—she didn't threaten to report us to the Historical Preservation Society for defacing a Victorian neighborhood or do the I'll-see-you-in-court routine. It was more like she was *sad* that her backyard view was about to be so unpleasantly modernized, and that she couldn't convince us to change our minds (at this point nearly all the poles were setting in concrete). By the end of the conversation I felt that she was disappointed in me and Mark personally. I actually felt bad about it—and we had never even seen her!

I apologized. Like the two thickheaded guys we were, it had never occurred to us to let our neighbors know we were putting up a fence on our property. Then I apologized for not having been more neighborly and introducing ourselves, but she told me it's customary for the old neighbors to welcome the new ones, and that she would have done just that once upon a time, but now she was "pretty much of a recluse."

"Well, gee," I said. "Could I—"

"No, no," said Mrs. McGuire. "No . . ." Her voice faded,

and after a moment she said, "Good-bye," and hung up.

Mark thought we should bring her a basket of fruit or some flowers or something, but I told him she'd made it very clear that she didn't socialize, not even a little bit.

She wasn't kidding. On weekends she let Byron out only after the girls (now including Gracie) were safely in the house, and the most we ever saw of her was a little bloused arm holding her back door open to let him in again. That was it. We never saw her leave the house; a landscaping crew did the yardwork, and groceries were delivered once a week and left on the porch. Her children might have visited her, but if they did, they were very quiet about it.

Byron, however, was another story. One of those little dogs who don't know how little they are, he liked to run around his yard and bark at the top of his apricot-size lungs. "Arf!" he would say, making the sound I always thought dogs make only in comic strips. "Arf arf!" And, just in case we hadn't understood, "Arf!"

"You know what he's doing, don't you?" Mark asked.

"Uh, barking?" Marlin Perkins had nothing on me.

"He's telling the whole neighborhood that Mrs. McGuire's

not alone. He's standing guard." As we looked out the kitchen window to see all twelve pounds of Byron scaring off the enemy, we both burst out laughing.

"He's not my first-draft pick for a watchdog," I said. "But he must know what he's doing. Nobody's given her any grief since we've been here."

Mark pulled a guilty look. "Nobody except us."

"Oh. Right."

But as the months passed and we heard nothing of the widow McGuire, and little of Byron, we pretty much forgot about them. Until—thanks to a yawning gap in Gracie's meager social life—we were reminded.

Gracie had continued growing at a tremendous rate, even with her fussy tastes and dainty appetite. I've mentioned that for the first few months her weight seemed to double every thirty days, but let me try to put her growth in perspective. While it takes the average human as long as sixteen or eighteen years to reach full size, a dog does it in *one* year. Even for a small dog, that's impressive; for a Great Dane, it's staggering. Factor in that a full-grown Great Dane at around 150 pounds is larger than many humans, and has grown to that size from about one pound at birth. Imagine a human growing to nearly full size and strength in a year's time, and you'll have some sense of the punishment the body of a Great Dane puppy goes through.

By now Gracie's head was just passing my waist (she stood about thirty inches at the shoulder), and her lean bone structure was equivalent to, say, a young human athlete's—without the body control. She was still as awkward as ever, easily faked out by the ever-mischievous (but no longer malicious) Dottie, and knocked herself over when her hind paws got ahead of her front paws. It was while she was in one of these graceful moments one autumn day, tackling a ladybug and trying to tame it as a pet, that Boston Byron was let out of his back door and immediately ran to the fence to greet her. He peered at her between the pickets and through the chain link and decided to use his best come-on line: "Arf!"

Short haired and full grown at a foot tall, Byron was mostly black but for white forelegs, a white snout, and a two-inch long white stripe extending from the top of his nose to the middle of his wrinkled forehead, giving him a look of perpetual curiosity that reminded me of Gracie. A very small Gracie.

The wrinkles (and the classification "canine") were where the resemblance ended, because Byron's thick trunk teetered on spindly legs (I hope he's not reading this) and his tiny snout was mashed in like a boxer's or pug's. Asleep under a tree, he snored like Santa on December 26; awake, he could outsnort a warthog.

Between them, it was fascination at first sight, sniffing at each other through the chain links and running up and down the fence in an effort to get closer. This remained their project for about a week. Dottie, at this point, was beginning to notice Gracie's absence. At least once I saw her attack a clump of grass near Gracie just to get her attention. It seemed she had gotten used to having Gracie as background music, but Gracie was singing her own song now.

I was in the yard watching Gracie and Byron one day when I saw Mrs. McGuire for the first time. She opened the door and called out to Byron to come in for dinner. As she scanned the yard to find him at the fence exchanging secrets with Gracie, our eyes met. I waved and smiled at her, but she started and quickly ducked back into the house like a turtle pulling its head in.

I was struck by her appearance. She was little—barely five feet tall, and thin, though not unhealthy looking. What really got me, though, was how put together she was. I guess I'd imagined that people who isolate themselves don't spend much time on their appearance, but she looked like she had just come back from a day of teaching circa 1955: a pressed white blouse and gray skirt, sensible shoes, reading glasses hanging from a silver chain, and a good half mile of white hair swept up and pinned Gibson-girl style. Did she go to all that effort simply to hang out with Byron all day? Should I have been making myself more presentable for Gracie?

I could just make out her shadow behind the storm door. "They're great friends," I shouted, pointing to Byron and Gracie. She took another step back. Byron, to his credit, proved my point by staying right where he was. I tried to think of something else to say, but I realized that my seeing her must be making her very uncomfortable, so I went back into the house. I looked out the kitchen window and, sure enough, the moment she heard our door slam the white-sleeved arm held her door open and the quavery voice called, "Byron! Dinnertime, dear! Din-ner!"

Byron may have been in love, but he wasn't rude, and at this second call he excused himself from Gracie's company and trotted back inside with a resounding "Arf!" that I took to mean *On my way, dear lady.* Or something like that—canine translation is still an imprecise science.

The next day, out of the blue, Gracie took up a new hobby: archaeology.

"Isn't it possible she's just digging up the lawn?" Mark stood at the kitchen door, watching her move earth.

"Sure," I said. "But since it's Gracie, I like to give her the benefit of the doubt."

I was right to suspect something more than diggity-dog instinct, but it took a few days to figure out what. In the meantime I didn't want her to turn the backyard into an excavation site, so I went out to "the dig" (that's archaeologist talk for "a big hole"), pointed into the hole, got in Gracie's face, and shouted "NO!" very severely, disapproving with every ounce of my being. She must have gotten the point, because she looked sheepish and ran away, and I didn't see her until dinner.

Unlike most dogs (and children, and probably grown-ups, for that matter), Gracie has a good memory for rules: If you chastise her for something once, she's very unlikely to do the same thing again. So I was pretty surprised when I caught her the next day beside a brand-new hole, panting and smiling at me. I looked around and saw several other holes of various sizes scattered around the yard. I wondered if maybe she thought I disapproved only of the *old* hole (its shape, its depth, its composition), but these *new* ones were so good I'd have to love them. I tried again, putting enough volume into my "NO!" that she must have felt its vibrations even if she wasn't scared by the angry face I put on to make the point.

This time the message really got through. She whimpered pathetically and ran back into the house, hiding behind the couch and refusing to come out, even when I crouched down and signaled to her that dinner was ready.

By morning we seemed to have made up, but the next time I let her out into the backyard, I decided to watch from the window. The minute she met Byron by the fence and greeted him, she promptly began digging. She was throwing earth with such force and focus that something told me to wait and see what unfolded.

Before this there had been no pattern to the holes around the yard. They were everywhere, some just scratching the grass loose, some wide, others narrow but no more than a few inches deep.

But this new hole surpassed the others in size in only a few seconds. Gracie was excavating furiously, tearing at the earth with both forepaws and sending the loosened soil flying in an arc between her hind legs and up in the air into a growing hill behind her. Byron was wagging his tail so hard that his hind legs kept bouncing up off the ground. Excited as he was, though, not a single "Arf!" escaped him—nothing more than the panting that accompanied his dancing pink tongue. I glanced quickly at the other house to see if Mrs. McGuire was watching. This time I was on Gracie's side.

In a few minutes she had torn the ground loose about six inches deep right against the fence. She'd have to dig ten times that if she wanted to get through. But instead, when the hole was deep enough, she swiped at the fence a few times to signal Byron. Without a moment's hesitation he dropped his little body into the hole and wiggled himself through.

I looked around the yard to take in the full scope of Gracie's project. Son of a gun! She had actually planned this. The scattered holes were just tests to build her skill and technique and to see how long she could dig before getting caught.

Somewhere along the way she'd figured out that she could dig a hole for Byron to come into her yard faster than she could dig one for her to invade his.

And here they were in front of me, rolling all over each other, panting and licking each other's faces. Then she did something I felt a little embarrassed to witness: they started to play tag and she let Byron catch her.

Now I made sure I let Gracie out into the backyard every evening as soon as I got home from work; if Byron wasn't there for his evening constitutional, he would be before long. On weekend days Gracie kept watch from the kitchen window, and when Byron was let out I waited a respectable three or four seconds for Mrs. McGuire to retreat to her shell before I opened the back door just in time to keep Gracie from scratching a hole through the wood. As soon as Byron saw her he burrowed through the leaves I had stuffed into the hole and began running around the yard with his pal. I had never seen Gracie so happy.

Most days they had a routine. First they would investigate every inch of the yard, starting with the same patch of grass each time, or chasing after wayward leaves. Sooner or later either Sarah or Dottie would appear on the scene. Early in the courtship Sarah—the shameless flirt—would initiate a game of tag, clearly trying to distract Byron from Gracie. Byron, faithful and chivalrous soul that he was, would indulge Sarah for a few minutes so as not to hurt her feelings, then go right back to Gracie's side. If the lovebirds were in a particularly mischievous mood, they'd find one of Dottie's toys—usually her beloved squeaky carrot—and bury it. Then they'd wait for her to come out and look for it, up to the point where she began her own frantic excavation of the yard. Invariably, though, Gracie would drag Dottie over and show her where the treasure was hidden—such a softie. I had heard dogs described as witty before, but these two had a fully evolved sense of humor. Not that it did my fledgling lawn any good.

Gracie had been fixed, so I wasn't worried about the possible problems of a mixed marriage and (gasp!) *medium-sized* offspring (not that I could imagine the logistics of conception— although if anyone could have orchestrated it, it would have been Gracie). But I was sure that Mrs. McGuire wouldn't approve of the match, so I played sentry as Gracie and Byron romped in the grass. Standing inside the back door, Mrs. M. couldn't see all of her own yard, let alone ours, so when she called to Byron he could tumble through the hole without her ever knowing that he had crossed into enemy territory. Once he was in his house, I stuffed the hole with leaves again. I knew I could keep this up until winter, when, if it came down to it, I would use snow.

Winter came early that year. By the end of November the winds cut through the bleak gray streets with a cruel harshness. Mark told me that Sarah and Dottie seemed disappointed at how few of their pals were showing up at the park on weekends—the owners silently declaring the weather too cold. And now Mrs. McGuire was letting Byron out less and less, usually restricting his supply of fresh air to five minutes in the morning and another five just before dinner. Gracie missed most of the morning airings and about half the evening ones—though when they did connect it was clear they were both overjoyed, at least until Mrs. McGuire's frail voice called Byron in to dinner. Then, one weekend, he didn't come out at all. Gracie spent most of both days in the yard, hanging her head the way she did when she was profoundly sad. And the following evening when I was getting back from work, I saw a bad sign. A very bad sign. It said FOR SALE and it was standing in Mrs. McGuire's front lawn.

When I got inside Gracie was curled up on the floor, forehead in full Great Dane wrinkle, letting out an occasional forlorn sigh. Impossible, I thought—how could she know? I got down next to her on the floor and saw that her eyes were wet. She knew. Don't ask me. Somehow, she knew.

I looked up Mrs. McGuire's number and called. No answer. I hated to disturb the sanctity of her solitude, but I went over and knocked on the door. Nothing. I tried again the next morning and the following afternoon, called various times during the day from the office, but still nothing. After a while I decided she must have just moved, and that's all, nothing more than that.

I wanted to help Gracie but I had no idea what to do. I let her out into the backyard. She stood at the fence. I tried to teach her new tricks. She lay on the ground and sniffled. I was ready to put an ad in the *Kansas City Star*. Svelte, sensitive, spayed female Great Dane seeks other dogs for fun, companionship, and yard work. Size not important.

Gracie's sadness began to slip into depression, and the dark gray skies weren't helping any. Instead of running around after Sarah and Dottie, she kept to herself, often lying on the floor and staring. And now that she was approaching her full size, instead of filling out she was getting thinner.

Sarah and Dottie, meanwhile, were shifting into their winter mode. In the warmer months they conserved their energy for the park, where they burned it off in quantities small countries would love to harness for their power needs. Now they just ran around the house, even Sarah—who, compared to Dottie, was inclined to be introspective. Pent up, Sarah was becoming even more analytical, staring at objects and taking them apart, as if she was trying to figure out how they worked. One night she lay on the remote control and turned on the TV. The look of revelation in her eyes was stunning: She had created light!

Dottie, the extrovert's extrovert, wasn't slowed by winter in the least. When it would have been time to go to the park on a warmer day, she simply acted like she was already there, suddenly deciding on a spot on the other side of the house where she *had* to be and racing there as fast as possible. I would sit in the kitchen over a bowl of Apple Jacks as she roared up from the distance, the rumble rising until she whizzed past me too fast for the naked eye to register, then disappeared, her presence evidenced only by the residue of black spots hanging in the air.

And my Gracie? Well, she lay on the floor at my feet, staring.

One slow-moving Saturday afternoon I opened the back door and leaned in the doorway, letting the harsh cold fill the already-drafty house. I was trying to figure out what to do with the trampled mess we were calling a backyard. Could anything ever grow there without all those paws stomping it into oblivion?

Just then, out of the corner of my eye, I spied a tiny white-bloused arm open Mrs. McGuire's back door, and a black-and-white cannonball shot out into the yard with enough force to knock over a regiment, had they been unlucky enough to stand in its path. It was Byron. And in case anyone had any doubts about his identity, he confirmed it for the neighborhood: "Arf! Arf arf! Arf arf arf arf!"

You may recall that Gracie is deaf. She can't hear. Sounds do not make their way into her perception. I was thinking, *Oh boy, won't she be surprised*—when I heard her tearing through the house like a tornado, humming in a rising roar as she got closer to the back door, "mmmm*mmmmmmMMMMMM!*" and flew out past me.

Byron, for his part, made a beeline for the fence and tunneled under. She collided with him and they toppled over, Byron making two tiny rolls to the side and Gracie an enormous flip, heels over head, and landing on her back. He leaped over her chest and licked her face. As she got back to her feet, Byron ran back and forth under her legs, his tiny ears barely reaching her knees. She nudged him with her snout and knocked him over again. Then it was my turn to be knocked over—Mrs. McGuire came out of the house.

She was wearing a long black wool winter coat with a little fur collar, the kind that might have been worn to great effect at the 1962 Christmas party, and black leather gloves. She must have been cold even with the coat and gloves, because she was holding herself and shivering, but she didn't seem to mind. She stepped far enough into the yard to watch the dogs, and unless she was wincing, she was smiling. Smiling away at Gracie and Byron together.

I went out into the yard, slowly, kicking some leaves so I wouldn't startle her, and she turned to me, still smiling.

"Mrs. McGuire?" I don't know where I get this uncanny ability to state the obvious. It's just a gift.

"Yes, dear."

"Hi, I'm Dan. We talked on the—"

"Yes, dear, I recognize your voice. You really should be wearing a coat."

"A coat? Oh, yeah, I will in a second. Listen, I just wanted to—" I broke off as I realized that she *really* wanted me to go get a coat. She was still smiling, but I could tell she expected her words to be obeyed. I made the universal *gimme-a-minute* sign, ran into the house, threw on a coat, and ran back, zipping up. I knew instinctively that she'd never let me get away with wearing it open.

She seemed pleased. "Now what was it you wanted to say?"

"Well, I, uh, ma'am, I just wanted to say I'm sorry about the hole, and I'll be happy to come over and fill it in for you. It's just, you know these dogs, I mean how they just love to dig . . . ma'am."

She was smiling again, her bright blue eyes almost as light as Gracie's. "I don't think that's a very good idea. If you did that, how would these two lovebirds ever see each other?"

A cold breeze blew just then, but I felt like the clouds had parted and the sun was shining through.

"Oh good! You mean, you don't mind about—?" I gestured to Byron and Gracie, who were now terrorizing a deflated football into silent submission.

She smiled at the question. "Oh heavens no, why should I mind? Isn't it hard enough to find love in this world, without having others put up obstacles for you?"

I didn't know what to say. Luckily, she did.

"You'll catch a terrible chill in this weather without a scarf, dear. Why don't you, um—" She suddenly looked nervous, like she'd forgotten her lines, then: "Oh, why don't you come over for a cup of tea? It would do us *both* good." Chances are I would have said yes to any neighbor, to be polite, but I was so curious about Mrs. McGuire—and especially her sudden change of character—that I couldn't possibly refuse.

Her home was everything ours would never be, even in a hundred years. The wood shone, the silver sparkled—even the tea service between us gleamed like nothing I've ever owned. But at the same time, the house seemed too big for her. And it was. It was hard for her to get up and down the stairs, and her children had finally convinced her to move into an assisted-living community, where she'd have her own apartment but be able to get help if she ever needed it. That's where she had been for the last two weeks, visiting with her children's families and choosing a new home—for the first time in fifty-four years.

"Wow," I said, brimming with insight. "That's a long time to be in one place."

She laughed. A sweet laugh, like water pouring into a glass. "Oh, Mr. McGuire, may he rest in peace, would have laughed at that. He was born in this house, lived his whole life here, and died here. Except for vacations, the only time he didn't live here was in the war." She looked into my eyes and guessed my question. "The Great War, dear." A smile. "When he brought me here after our honeymoon, I thought I'd never get over feeling like a guest. And when he . . . left me here, October 16, 1978, I didn't want to be anywhere else. Ever." Her eyes misted. "And it was so easy not to leave. The children were far away, all my friends had moved or passed . . . and then last week my youngest granddaughter, Emily, said to me, 'Nana, I order you to make friends!'"

We both burst out laughing.

"Can you imagine that—four years old and 'I *order* you,' she told me! Then she said, 'Besides, it's good practice for when you move to your new house. You can't just hang out with Byron all day!'"

We laughed again, but suddenly it hit me: Byron would be joining her.

She sighed. "You know, dear, that was my one reservation. I hate to take him away from his new friend, but—"

I was about to say that I understood, but she finished her sentence.

"—he's my only friend."

Oh. Now I understood. Now I really understood. Gracie had her whole life ahead of her to make more friends, but for Mrs. McGuire there was only Byron. He was the most recent in a proud line of Boston terriers who had graced the McGuire household for many years—his predecessors, as you might have guessed, were named Shelley, Keats, and Dickens ("Our daughter was tired of poets")—but he was also the end of the line for her. "I hope he outlives me," she said, "because I couldn't do without him. But then I chide myself for thinking so selfishly, because if I'm gone, who will take care of *him?*"

There's no such thing as a loving relationship between animal and person that isn't special, but hearing Mrs. McGuire talk about Byron I realized that the bond between a pet and an elderly person is unique. I can't explain why; maybe it's because the elderly have a perspective on mortality that allows them to appreciate other lives in a way the rest of us can't. Whatever it is, since knowing Mrs. McGuire it's always struck me that older people cherish their pets in a way that makes children's love of pets seem almost pale by comparison.

The nice news, for Gracie and me, was that Byron and Mrs. McGuire wouldn't be leaving for another couple of months.

And before they did I was sure that, somehow, Byron would explain to Gracie that his sticking with his human was a far, far better thing than he had ever done before. And that, somehow, Gracie would understand.

eight

The Gracious Gourmet

"The worst thing is that big dogs just don't live a long time. There are always exceptions, but mostly the rule is, the bigger the dog, the shorter the life." It was the Monday after Thanksgiving, we were on a rare coffee break at the office, and the new secretary had just asked Anne what the worst thing was about having a Great Dane. "Plenty of them don't make it to their sixth birthday!" I must have had a stricken look on my face, because she zeroed in on me and added, "But lots of them live to nine or even ten!"

I know she meant to encourage to me, but it didn't really work, especially because I was already worried about Gracie making it to age two. It had become clear that we could no longer laugh about what a finicky eater she was, or how she was naturally svelte: She was so underweight we could see her ribs, and at this point if she wasn't anorexic, she was close. But weight wasn't the only problem: Even though her bones were almost full grown, if she didn't get the nutrition she needed she could wind up with crippling bone and joint problems. Now that Mark and I had finally acknowledged the obvious, we were frantic to figure out what we could do to get Gracie to fatten up. Or even eat! Over the next couple of weeks we tried everything we could think of.

First we changed dog food. We had always fed the girls the doggy equivalent of what we ate ourselves, which meant they generally subsisted on generic foodlike products that were filling but didn't really taste good. Up to this point we'd been reluctant to support the biggest pet food company in the universe, because we assumed the extra cost was paying for their ads and packaging, but this was for Gracie. We set our politics aside and bought a few cans of the big-market brand—the one you would have wanted your mother to get when you were a kid, because Lorne Greene told you to in the commercial.

Well, Sarah and Dottie couldn't get enough of that brand-name stuff. Unfortunately, Gracie could; she could get enough without having a second mouthful. And Sarah and Dottie, charter members of the Clean Plate Club, were only too happy to help Gracie clean hers. I knew something was *really* wrong because Gracie no longer tried to stop them.

So we tried the high-end dog food. You know the one—its containers are all made from recycled products, and its contents are

100 percent actual food. It even smells good when you open the can. I was going to say something like, "Poor people all over the world would probably be happy to eat this stuff," but then I remembered that we weren't so well off ourselves: I have to admit that the idea was a little tempting to *us*. We were alone in being tempted, though—me, Mark, Sarah, and Dottie. Gracie couldn't have been less interested if it was still in the can.

So we went deluxe. The fancy-schmancy pet care store downtown (where we had never shopped because we were afraid we'd have to show our tax returns to get in) sold an all-organic, multigrain, hypo-allergenic, vegetarian dog chow that, they assured us, would do the trick. "It had better," Mark muttered. "A week of this stuff for Gracie costs half the food budget for *us*." I hoped that somehow Gracie would understand how much we'd spent on this extra-special food and give it a chance: *Aw, the guys are really bending over backward to make me happy, so I'll chow down just to let 'em know I appreciate the effort.*

I must have been sending very powerful psychic vibes,

because she actually considered this one: She took one tiny mouthful, chewed it forty-five times as if she were worried there might be glass in it, and, finally, swallowed. Then she picked up another couple of morsels and, sooner or later, swallowed them too. Then . . . she sighed and walked away.

Mark smacked his brow. "Could you please explain to me how you managed to pick out the only anorexic Great Dane in the entire history of dogdom?"

I knelt next to Gracie and gave her a big hug, which she reciprocated but almost without conviction. "You're not anorexic, are you, sweetheart? You wouldn't break my heart like that, would you?"

"This is insane." Mark shook his head. "She's gonna be on intravenous feeding in about a week. We have to do something!" For the first time I could tell that he was as worried about Gracie as I was.

Well, yeah, obviously we had to do something. But what?

We both pondered for a minute, anxiously eyeing Gracie's prominent ribs. At the same time we both said, "Dr. Benjamin!"

"I'll call him first thing tomorrow."

"Call him now and leave a message with his service."

Well, this was Dr. Benjamin, so when I dialed the after-hours number recited on his office answering machine, I didn't get a service. I got his home.

"Uh, hi. I'm sorry to bother you, but is Dr. Benjamin there?"

"No, he's not. Can I give him a message?"

I explained everything that was going on with Gracie, feeling guilty the whole time that I hadn't waited to call him in the morning, but knowing I was really too worried to wait. It turned out I was talking to the vet's daughter, who had just stopped by to feed and play with the dogs—Dr. and Mrs. Benjamin were visiting their son and his family in Denver.

"Oh." Sinking feeling. "Well, um, is there a covering doctor I can—"

"There *is* a covering doctor, but why don't you call Dad first and see what he says?"

"Oh, I couldn't do that."

"Oh, sure you could!"

"No, I really couldn't."

She laughed. "No, you don't understand. If you *don't* call him, I'm gonna get in big trouble, okay?"

Naturally I didn't want to get her in trouble, so I took the number and called Dr. Benjamin in Denver. His son, who sounded just like him minus the gravel in the voice, put him on immediately. From the good doctor's tone, you would have thought he was waiting for my call.

"Oh, poor little Miracle," he said, after I told him what was going on. "She's never had it easy, has she?"

I'd never thought about it that way before. I'm embarrassed to say it, but this was the first time I thought about how all this eating trouble might be for *Gracie*. I mean, of course I was worried about her physical well-being, but it had never occurred to me that my beloved animal friend had emotions about herself. She might be in discomfort or even physical pain. She *had* to be hungry. And she was probably scared—why wouldn't she be? *I* had feelings about being sick when I just caught a cold. And to make matters worse, she had no way of understanding what was wrong with her. When I thought about this, I wanted all the more urgently for her to get better. Dr. Benjamin wanted the same thing.

"Hmm. We have a ten o'clock flight back tomorrow morning . . . Bring Gracie in around one so I can have a talk with her and run a few tests." I felt better just hearing him say this—she would be in the hands of an expert, science would take care of her, and everything would be okay. "But I'm curious," he continued. "Have you tried cooking for her yourself?"

What kind of a question was that? "No, I . . . I mean, I don't really cook for *myself* more than spaghetti and burgers and stuff like that. I can grill on the barbecue, but I'm not exactly the Galloping Gourmet."

"That's putting it mildly," said Mark from the sidelines. Like he could brag—just because *he* knew how to make spaghetti, burgers, and *pancakes*.

"And neither is my roommate," I finished, giving Mark the evil eye.

"Actually," said Dr. Benjamin, "you don't need to be. If you can read a recipe, you can make her simple things from almost any cookbook, so long as you don't use sugar or salt or chocolate. Dogs like garlic, believe it or not, but anything you make from whole grains and fresh ingredients can only do them good. Organic vegetables if you can afford 'em—animals don't need additives or chemicals any more than we do."

"Yeah, but Dr. Benjamin, you don't understand. I *really* don't know how to cook!"

"Well, then this is a good time to learn, isn't it?" He didn't wait for me to answer. "Start simple, but be creative. Experiment!"

Be creative. Experiment. Easy for him to say. On the other hand, as Mark said, "She can't eat any less than she does now."

So that was it, then. We had no choice but to try. And hope we came up with the formula before it was too late.

The next day Dr. Benjamin confirmed in person that Gracie's low weight could affect her bones and her general health as she got older. But he couldn't find anything physically wrong with her, and I think he checked for everything under the sun. "Try home cooking, son. You'd be amazed at the ills it can cure."

So I did. I had taken the afternoon off to bring Gracie in, and she and I went straight from Dr. Benjamin's to the library (one of us stayed in the car) and took out a half-dozen cookbooks—for humans, since as far as I could tell nobody had ever written a cookbook for dogs. We went from there to the local health food store and picked up a pound each of four different kinds of whole-grain flour, along with carrots, garlic, spinach, apples, peanut butter and honey. I had no idea what I was going to make, but I sure hoped it would be good. I hoped it could be recognized as food.

Once I got in the door and set the bags down, though, I lost all the momentum that panic had generated: What *was* I going to make? As I flipped through the cookbooks, waiting for something to jump out and say, "I am the recipe that will save Gracie's life," I heard Dr. Benjamin's voice echoing, "Start simple." What's simple if you've never really cooked? I drummed my fingers on the kitchen table, and Gracie came in from the other room as quickly as if I had called her. Simple. Hmm. I would have to resort to my secret weapon.

"Midwestern-Company-good-afternoon-how-may-I-direct-your-call-today?"

"Ahem." I made my voice rough and gravelly. "Yes, this is Mr. Hassenfeffermessen. I'd like to speak with Anne."

"What was that name again?"

"Anne, please!"

"Uh, yessir!"

"This is Anne."

I whispered. "It's me. I have an important question. How do you cook?"

Anne snorted. "You are a deeply troubled human being." I heard her cover the phone, and then her muffled voice saying, "No, it's okay, it's a friend of mine."

I whispered, "*Mr. Hassenfeffermessen.*"

"Mr. Hassen—oh, be quiet, you goofball! Now, what's the problem?"

"Okay, see, Dr. Benjamin tells me there's nothing physically wrong with Gracie's digestive processes as far as he can tell, and he thinks what she really needs is to have fresh home cooking instead of any of the packaged junk 'cause she might just have a sensitive stomach, so I swing by Go to Health and pick up like, I don't know, maybe four different kinds of flour and some spinach and garlic and apples and stuff only no sugar or salt or chocolate, and I hit the library to get some real basic cookbooks and they don't have anything on cooking for dogs or any other animals for that matter, which is insane, and now I'm home and I'm trying to figure out what I oughta make for her and it's gotta be something really simple and I open up the simplest cookbook and I'm all ready to get in there to save my little girl's life and then I remember *I don't know how to cook!*"

Anne didn't say anything for a few seconds after my explanation. Then, "I see. You're sure you didn't leave anything out?"

"No," I said, panting. I swallowed hard. "That's pretty much it."

"Okay. Something simple. How about cookies?"

"Cookies?"

"Yup."

"For a dog?"

"That's right."

"Dog cookies?"

"Is there static on the line? *Dog, Cookies!*"

"Yeah, but why would—"

"Look, Chef Boy-Ar-Dee, you need to make something simple. There's nothing simpler than cookies. How many times do you see me bring cookies into the office?"

"Just about every week, I'd say."

"That's right, and I'm not staying up all night to do it. So just find the simplest cookie recipe in the simplest book, and if it says sugar or salt or chocolate just leave 'em out, and you're all set!"

"Uh-huh. How do you know which one is the simplest?"

She inhaled deeply. "It has the fewest ingredients, and the shortest instructions."

"Right. Okay. I think I got it. No problem. Thanks a lot. See you tomorrow."

My momentum was building again. I found a recipe for cookies that had only about four ingredients; it called for apple juice as a sweetener. What could be simpler than that? Well, probably nothing, though you'd be surprised how easy it is for a non-cook to mess up the simplest recipe in the book. Especially if the paw of a curious Great Dane sweeps a bag of flour off the counter and onto an equally curious but shorter Dalmatian, who loses half her spots and leaves white paw tracks over every reachable surface in the house. That's when Mark decided to call.

"Hey, I just called your office to see what's up with Gracie, and Anne told me all about it. She said you're gonna be cooking—" He might have had more to say, but he was laughing too hard.

"Yeah, very funny."

"Hey, I have an idea—why don't you just give the cookbook to Gracie? Cut out the middleman!" More laughter.

"All right, laughing boy. If you know so much, what's 'sifting' mean?"

He tapered off. "What do you—heh-heh—what do you mean?"

"'Sift four cups flour.' What's 'sift'?"

"Oh, okay. Sifting. That's when you, uh, you sort of go through the flour and you see if anything doesn't look right—

y'know, like pebbles, or dirt, or something like that—and you just pick it out of the flour."

"Oh. Really?"

"Yeah, my mom does it all the time. Sifting. You gotta do it with rice, too—sift out all the . . . junk, basically."

"Hmm." Maybe Mark *did* know more about cooking than I did. I scanned down the recipe for other words. "Okay, what about 'folding'?"

"'Folding'? Um, in what sense, exactly?"

"'Fold half cup butter into flour in medium mixing bowl.'"

"Right. Okay, now, 'folding,' when it comes to butter, is basically, you take a stick of butter, right? And you cut it into really thin slices, okay? And then you just fold the slices very neatly, so it doesn't take up a lot of space in the mix—" He might have gone on with me diligently taking notes if he hadn't exploded laughing again.

"No problem," I said. "When I graduate from the Cordon Bleu and open up my own four-star restaurant, I'm gonna remember this day. You just come around the back door after closing every night, and I'll let you have whatever's not good enough for us to give to the stray cats." Instead of waiting for Mark to catch his breath, I hung up the phone and called the best cook I know: my sister, Theresa.

Luckily Theresa was up on the latest culinary techniques, like sifting and folding and other things too technical to explain here. Suffice it to say that, once I had run out and bought a sifter for seventy-nine cents and two cookie trays for a dollar fifty each, I had all the ingredients, equipment, and information I needed. Which is why it's so hard to understand how my efforts produced such lousy results. I should have paid more attention in my high school Bachelor Living class.

The first batch looked just terrible—split, cracked, and bubbled. They looked less like cookies than rock samples from the moon. You wouldn't feed them to your *dog!*

Just to show I wasn't holding out on her, I plopped down onto a chair and held the dismal results out to Gracie. "I'm sorry, sweetie. I don't know the first thing about cooking. I couldn't bake a freakin' cupcake if I had a team of chefs walking me through it step by step." I stroked her forehead. "I don't know what I'm gonna do, girl. How am I ever gonna get you to eat before it's too late?"

Gracie approached the hand holding the fossilized cookie, gave her customary thanks, and slurped up the little cookie. I tried to coax her into giving it back—I hadn't meant for her to *eat* it!—but nothing doing. She chewed it a little, cocked her head to one side like she was sloshing a fine vintage over her tongue, chewed it some more, and finally swallowed. I waited for her to turn and walk away, her trademark sign that the food has not passed muster. She stood right there. But she didn't open her mouth to show me that she wanted another, she just kept looking at me. *Okay,* I thought, gazing into her baby blues. *You're not walking away, you're not asking for more . . . are you telling me to keep trying?* She didn't look away, didn't even blink, so I took that as a yes or at least a *What else ya got?* I washed out all the bowls and set to making another batch, determined not to burn this one. Gracie stayed in the kitchen beside me.

There was no window in the oven door, so I ended up checking the second batch every five minutes or so—just often enough to make the process take fifteen minutes longer than it should have, but not often enough to catch it before half the cookies were black-bottomed. I took the tray out to cool, drumming my fingers, while Gracie stood patiently. After a minute I blew on one of the unburned ones, and offered it to her.

She thanked me, took it up, chewed, cocked her head, chewed, chewed some more, swallowed . . . And? She opened her mouth—not wide, the way she would for something scrumptious, but just wide enough to tell me she'd try another. My heart was beating fast. I gave her another: thanks, chew, tilt, chew, chew, swallow . . . closed mouth. Closed mouth, but not going anywhere.

I held her head in both hands. "Gimme a hint—more butter? Less garlic? Too crunchy? Not sweet enough?" She wouldn't give me half a clue; she wanted me to figure it out myself. *All right, fine—I will!* But not that evening. And not the next one, either, though I kept trying, and Sarah and Dottie were perfectly happy to eat most of my attempts (Dottie would have wolfed down Mark's socks if they were sprayed with Eau de Liver Pâté). But Gracie never walked away. Did she get that I was trying hard? Did she *know* I'd eventually get it right? Whatever the reason, she was there three nights later when I got it—an entire tray, golden brown top and bottom, not raw in the middle, not too soft. It felt right, but there was only one way to know.

I held one out. Thanks, slurp, chew, swallow, mouth wide open. *Mouth wide open?* I gave her another one: same thing. Another: same. It was traveling down her throat before I had it settled in my palm. I was so happy I almost cried; I looked up at the ceiling and thanked God, something I hadn't done in a very long time. Gracie did the same, in her own way: She ate another cookie.

I kissed her all over her big beautiful furry face. She had done it again—she picked up my assumptions and turned them around completely. I was convinced that I couldn't cook, could never learn to cook, and anyway if she wouldn't eat any of the high-class canine cuisine we had bought for her already, she was never gonna eat any concoction of mine.

But I was wrong. She was willing to eat what I made for her—the third day I'd ever baked in my life. And unless she just liked to suffer, she really *liked* my cooking! She hadn't given up on herself, or me; and when I took just a half step to meet her, she came the rest of the way to me.

I put Gracie's paws on my shoulders and started singing, "We are the champions, we are the champions . . . of the world!" Sarah and Dottie came in to find out what all the excitement was about. Dottie leaped up and pulled the tray of cookies off the table and onto the floor, where all three of them—Sarah, Dottie, *and* Gracie—dove in to devour the spoils. And Gracie, bless her heart, nosed Dottie away from *her* share.

nine

My First Christmas

My parents split up the year I turned twelve, and after that I always had to divide Christmas Day between them. That's why, when I was talking to my mom on December 18 and she said she'd be spending the holidays with her husband's family in South Carolina, I was almost relieved. For the first time in ages I wouldn't have to make one of those awkward midday departures from my dad, and we "kids" wouldn't have to divvy up the day in parental shifts. But when Theresa called to remind me that she and the kids were taking my dad to share Christmas with the newest grandchild at my brother Gerard's place in Bonner Springs, I felt like the Grinch had stolen my Christmas.

I hung up the phone and announced, "Bah, humbug!" to the empty kitchen. The truth was, I had always dreaded Christmas. I know that's the exact wrong spirit to have, but as the youngest of five kids in a house where money was tight if it was there at all, I discovered pretty early that this wonderful day could be filled with tension and conflict. It wasn't about not getting presents I had my heart set on, or not getting the "better" presents my brothers got—just about every kid deals with that. It was other things that were harder to name. Maybe some of it was my mom and dad's regret that there couldn't be more or better gifts. But no, that wasn't it either. For as far back as I can remember I felt like I was missing out on something—something wonderful.

It wasn't about gifts or anything specific; more the hope, even the yearning, that "things" would be good this year. That somehow it would be my wonderful Christmas at last, when no one would pick on me but no one would ignore me, and I could have as much of everything as I wanted (seconds, thirds, even *fourth* helpings of stuffing!). And that I wouldn't feel lonely at the end of the day—lonelier than I ever did on days that weren't supposed to be special.

After my parents' divorce it seemed like every other year one of my siblings was leaving home. Finally it was just me and my dad left alone in a house once brimming over with kids, and my brothers and sister felt like visitors at Christmas. Then when I went off to college we were *all* guests in the house, and even though there were also girlfriends and boyfriends, then wives, husbands, and kids . . . well, it was never a Very Brady Christmas. Maybe I was asking for the moon—that sense of "loving home and family" that I always thought I was supposed to have. Actually, the one that I always thought everyone else had.

And now, this year, there wasn't going to be *any* Christmas at the family homestead. My brother Tim was taking his family to his in-laws, Anne was taking her kids to her parents' home in St. Joe, and Mark was doing the family thing at his folks' place. *Nice going, Scrooge*, I thought. *You've been griping about Christmas for almost thirty years, and now you get to spend it by yourself. I hope you're satisfied.*

Well, I wasn't satisfied, but I was busy and determined to stay that way. Since I had discovered that the way to Gracie's stomach was through her . . . stomach, I was on what I can only describe as a baking binge. Granted, my entire repertoire consisted of cookies, but if I do say so myself, what cookies!

The moment I achieved even general competence (meaning I stopped burning entire batches—my mantra was *golden brown*), I started to get experimental. Very experimental. Basically, I wanted to see what good foods I could put in a cookie that would still look and feel like a cookie, yet taste good to Gracie. I tried just about any nonmeat, nonchocolate, nonsalt, nonsugar ingredient I could find to spice it up. Some of the add-ins were obvious for cookies but others weren't. All three dogs loved garlic (who knew?), and Gracie pretty consistently enjoyed carrots and spinach, with bananas and apples running a close second.

I tried not to take it personally when Gracie didn't like a batch, and once I realized I didn't have to worry that she would stop eating again—whatever she liked once, she kept on liking—I felt free to experiment. That's how I learned that Gracie did *not* appreciate pears. When she bit into a cookie with pear in it, she'd squint her eyes, raise her lips off her teeth like curtains, shake her head vigorously, and say (I'm quoting), "*Brrrrrrr!* Brack! Brack!" I was happy to learn later that other dogs weren't so picky.

Mark and I had decided to have a New Year's Eve party, but as usual we hadn't done anything to prepare for it—that just wasn't our style. So I was a little surprised one mid-December day when Mark picked up a garlic and spinach cookie, sniffed it, and said, "Hey, what if you baked up a few batches of these for New Year's?"

I gave him the have-you-thought-about-seeking-professional-help look he likes to give me. "Mark, nobody's gonna eat these! They're for dogs!"

He fumed—just one fume, but a powerful one. "I *meant* for dogs, you nutcase."

"We're gonna invite people's *dogs* to the party?"

"No, well, yeah, I mean, we *could,* but that's not the point. I was just thinking that since practically everybody we know has a dog, it'd be cool to give out a little bag of New Year's dog cookies as treats." He stared at me. "For their *dogs.*"

"Huh. I'll think about it." Actually, I was already thinking about it, and I thought it was a great idea, but you can't give a guy like Mark too much credit or it goes straight to his head.

"Hey, you oughta make a batch for your dad's dog and take it over for Christmas."

"Oh, I'm not going there for Christmas." I told him the whole story about why I wouldn't be spending the day with my family this year.

He looked perplexed. "So then where *are* you going for Christmas?"

"Ah, I was gonna hang out with the girls, maybe go to a movie, bake some more cookies . . ."

"Um, no." That look again. "I seriously don't think so."

"What do you mean?"

"I mean I seriously don't think you're hanging out here by yourself instead of coming over to my parents' house for Christmas."

"Come on, Mark, I can't come over to your family thing."

"Why not?"

"You know—it's Christmas! It's a family meal. Maybe *the* family meal. I'm not family. It wouldn't be right."

Mark rolled his eyes and smiled at the same time. "For a guy with a good Catholic education, you have some strange ideas about Christmas. But I have to say, you have some *really* strange ideas about family." He stood up from the kitchen table and looked all around him, almost like he was noticing the house for the first time.

"Look at this." He was gesturing toward everything: The mess on the counter, the piles of newspaper, the three goofy looking dogs who had come in to be part of the conversation. "*Look* at all this. Look at these knuckleheads." He pointed at the girls, who started going for his hand. "This place. Everything it took to get it. Everything it takes to keep it. Every penny we had, and most of the ones we'll ever have for years. Every day we hang out—the repairs, the laundry, dinner, TV, the dogs. This is family. *This.*" He waved his arms like a storefront preacher. "It's not somewhere else, or some other time, or some other person. Yeah, sure, it's the people who raised you and the ones you grew up with. But it's also whoever you live side by side with, day in and day out. It doesn't matter if it's college, or the army, or—" *big* sweeping gesture "—*this,* or whatever! That's family. *We're* family. And if I can't bring my family to Christmas, now *that* just wouldn't be right."

I couldn't argue with that. Not that I wanted to. To tell the truth, it was an argument I felt kind of honored to lose.

Christmas morning was cold and clear—one of those days when the world is in sharper focus. We loaded the girls into Mark's truck (Christmas without dogs? I don't think so!) and drove out to his parents' place in Leawood—a pretty house on the right side of the tracks. I didn't know what to expect. All I knew was that his dad, Gerald, was incredibly smart and had started his own pharmaceutical research company, where Mark worked; and his mom, LuAnn, was very nice—not only a great cook, but the perfect mom.

It was the strangest Christmas of my life: Nothing happened. Nothing happened, and it couldn't have felt better. Everybody welcomed us, dogs included. LuAnn acted like I'd been on the guest list for months. "Dan, thank goodness you're here!"

Since Mark's family lived in a nice part of town, I figured the ritual exchange of gifts would be a kind of can-you-top-this game, and I'd want to hide in a corner because I didn't have any gifts to give or get. But I figured wrong—there *was* no ritual exchange of gifts. Of course there were fun things for the kids, a big toy and a small toy each, and Mark and his brothers had chipped in on a piece of artwork for their parents' home. Aside from that there was just a string of old-fashioned red felt stockings hanging on the mantel, one for each member of the—

"Now, Dan, here's yours, next to Mark's. Don't spill it."

A Christmas stocking. I had a Christmas stocking. Mark's mom had made a stocking for me. With my name on it, in glue and glitter. I was thirty years old and I felt like I was ten, getting a stocking. It was a nice feeling.

"Hey, what didja get?" I followed the voice down to see Mark sitting cross-legged on the floor next to his five-year-old niece Laura, slowly emptying his stocking's contents into his lap, while she did the same with hers. I leaned over to check out Mark's spoils.

It was a wonderfully peculiar combination of the practical, the indulgent, and the silly: a pack of six white monogrammed handkerchiefs, a little plastic mesh bag of foil-wrapped chocolates, a flip-book of pictures of a horse and rider going over a series of hurdles, a nice necktie, a pack of football cards, a Santa Claus Pez dispenser . . . He kept shaking the stocking, and the stuff just kept coming out. Finally, he got to the bottom of it.

"Wait a sec, what's this?" He pulled out what looked like a cookie cutter in the shape of a dog bone, rubber-banded to a little piece of paper. "Hey, Mom—this should've gone in Dan's stocking!"

I started to say, "What is it—?"

"I know!" LuAnn yelled from the kitchen. "But his stocking was so full already, you boys'll just have to share it."

"Boy, I don't know," said Mark. "I might want it all for myself."

I snatched the paper out of his hand. "Let me see that." It

was a recipe for baking dog biscuits!

LuAnn came in, wiping her hands on a dishtowel. "Isn't it great? I found it in an old cookbook."

Dottie materialized out of nowhere and started trying to take the recipe from me—as if she somehow knew that the little scrap of paper meant food. Naturally, Gracie brought up the rear a second later, and I had to pocket the thing to make sure they didn't eat it before I could translate it into its proper form.

"Boys, I think they're trying to tell you something."

"I'm sure they can wait till I test it on them tomorrow." A bone-shaped cookie cutter. Huh.

"Well, I just took out the turkey, the pies are cooling on the racks, and everything else can wait until we can cut the bird, so the oven's yours to use. If the turkey turns out too dry, we may *all* be eating those biscuits!"

Mark was suddenly into it. "I'll give you a hand!"

Laura piped up. "Can I help?"

"Me too!" said Kaitlin, Laura's three-year-old sister. "I wanna help!"

Mark stood up and made a megaphone with his hands. "*Kht!* May I have your attention, please? Will all those who wish to participate in the baking of the Christmas dog biscuits please convene in the kitchen for further instructions. *Kht!*"

Unlike our kitchen back at the Rue Morgue, LuAnn's was

fully stocked and equipped. In the twenty minutes before the turkey was carved, we managed to whip up the recipe (using an electric mixer instead of a spatula!), roll it out nice and flat (instead of squashing it with a cookie sheet!), and cut out dozens of perfect little dog-bone-shaped biscuits. Sarah and Dottie stayed to watch the football game with Mark's dad and brother, but Gracie joined us. I'm sure she would have helped with the work if Laura and Kaitlin weren't hanging all over her, receiving Gracie facials, screaming "Eww!" and then running back for more. Laura had the honor of sliding the trays into the oven and Kaitlin got to press the oven light switch to make sure the biscuits were okay, just as LuAnn called us in.

Once everyone was seated at the table Mark's dad cleared his throat, the obvious signal that we should be quiet so he could say grace. "Ahem. Dan, would you like to say grace?"

Suddenly every eye at the table was on me, the way a dozen floodlights zero in on an escaping convict, pinning him against the wall. Actually, the eyes looked pretty friendly, as eyes go. "Uh, it's been a while . . ."

Chuckles all around. Mark stage-whispered to his mother, "He doesn't know how to say grace!"

"Of course he does," she assured him. And me.

Then it hit me that I'd *never* said grace before. Okay. No problem. "Um." *Good start, Dan, you're rolling already.* "God, thank you for the bounty of the meal we are about to eat in honor of this holy day. Thank you for the . . . the gift of love that you bestowed upon us, and all humankind, which we honor today. And thank you, God, for the precious gift of family and friends, through which we embody that love, today and—hopefully—every day. Amen."

"Amen."

I looked around to see if anyone was making a you-call-that-*grace?* face, but no one was.

Mark even looked impressed. "I guess the Jesuits knew what they were doing."

"That was lovely, Dan," said LuAnn. "Thank you."

"Very nice," Gerald said. "Let's eat!"

That *was* pretty impressive, I thought. I wonder where it came from? Just then I sensed a puff of moist air on my wrist and turned to see Gracie almost nose to nose with me, smiling. Her exquisite sense of smell had told her that the biscuits were done, and she knew I'd want to know. We trotted off to the kitchen together, and she tucked into her own dinner. "Bone appetit," I said, and returned to the table.

Then I ate. And ate. And ate. I got to have seconds of everything I wanted, and even thirds on the potatoes and the stuffing. Thanks to Laura and Kaitlin, the dogs got the best table scraps of their lives and were so full that they left enough biscuits for LuAnn to give her dog-owning friends the next day. After the meal, we did the strangest thing: we didn't turn on the TV. We talked.

We all talked, in groups, and pairs, and changing combinations throughout the day. After dessert I was so stuffed I couldn't move, so I sat in front of the fire in a digestive stupor, staring into the flames without a thought in my head beyond *Boy, am I stuffed!* Then Gracie, who may have had a full belly for the first time in her life, sat down next to me and licked my cheek. Just telling me that she was there, and that she was glad I was there too.

When Mark and I left with our canine crew, it struck me that I'd had the Christmas I always wished for—a Christmas where people mattered to each other.

People and dogs, of course.

ten

Auld Lang Syne

ven though I'd gone to sleep on December 30 still basking in the glow of my post-Christmas good spirits (and my ongoing relief at discovering the secret to feeding Gracie), I woke up the morning of New Year's Eve in a completely different state of mind. I couldn't tell what it was, but I knew it was different.

There are probably a lot of sensitive guys in the world who are in constant contact with their feelings, and they react accordingly. ("Yeah, I was having some feelings, so I talked them out with my inner child and now we're fine!") I envy guys like that. With me, emotions—except maybe fear—are more like conversations in the apartment next door: You can only hear them if they're loud, and even then you have to try hard to make out what's being said. Today I could have used some professional surveillance equipment.

At first it just felt like restlessness, even antsiness. I figured it was because I had a bunch of errands to run for the party that night, so I got rolling. Since Mark didn't have the day off, he let me borrow his truck, and I spent most of the morning and afternoon getting party supplies—with the company and moral support of Misses Sarah, Dottie, and Gracie. I had made a ridiculously detailed checklist (Bud—cans—2 cases; Bud—bottles—2 cases; chips—ridges—4 bags; chips—regular—4 bags . . .), thinking that as I checked off each item, I'd feel a little better. I kept checking 'em off, and the antsiness gave way to a feeling of intense heaviness—not like I'd just gained four hundred pounds (that would come later), but more like the earth's gravity had increased a few hundred percent and I was barely able to lug my own weight around. I'm just sensitive enough to know that the feeling was emotional, not physical, but when I pressed my ear against the wall between me and my feelings, all I could make out was a disgruntled growl.

But I had more pressing worries. As of thirty minutes before party time, I hadn't so much as shaved, showered, or dressed, let alone decorated or set up. Naturally, that's when my inner child decided to show up and tell me he had a sinking feeling that the party *could* have been great, but was now bound to be a huge disappointment to everyone—kind of a small-scale version of my life. I was just starting to glimpse the hairy green monster that had been sitting on my back all day when the doorbell rang. It was Anne—at the door, that is.

Whether it's for work or play, Anne is always the first one to arrive—this time it was with two trays of just-baked chocolate

chocolate-chip cookies, two shopping bags full of stuff, and Merlin, who cantered past me to butt heads with Gracie, his litter sister. Anne entered a little more gracefully than Merlin, her big smile all ready to tell me what a great job I'd done decorating. When she saw that by the looks of things it could just as easily have been April 28 or October 4, she took a deep breath and said, "Hey, party boy! I came by early to help you get the place ready!"

I narrowed my eyes at her. "No, you didn't."

She smiled even bigger, eyes bright enough to give a clear glimpse of the former prom queen. "Sure I did!"

"No you didn't. Admit it."

She was already taking off her coat and handing it to me, still beaming as she scoped out the state of the hovel and started rolling up her sleeves. "Sweetie, I came early 'cause I like your company for some strange reason, and I wanted to give you any kind of help you needed. Right about now you're probably thinking your life's going down the tubes and the party's gonna be a disaster, right?"

You know how sometimes when you're miserable a friend will get what's happening in your head, maybe even before you get it yourself, and you could almost cry?

Anne squeezed my shoulder. "Okay," she said. "Let's transform this place from Dog-and-Guyville to Party Central." Which we did, in less time than it takes most folks to hang a picture. Of course it helped that she'd brought along yards of tinsel, streamers, a bag of balloons, a couple of [drawing] dozen horns, and four long strings of moon-and-stars [drawing] lights that, combined with a dozen tea candles in little bowls of water, made the downstairs look [drawing] like a sky full of constellations had come inside. That, [drawing] and the fixings for some hors d'oeuvres that she "threw together" in about as long as it took me to open a bag of flour.

Mark managed to pull into the driveway in my Hyundai a solid minute before our first official guests arrived. He was greeted by Sarah, Dottie, Gracie, and Merlin, all of whom wanted some kind of attention from him, if not an actual autograph. Mark pushed his way through the canine throng, saying, "Sorry, folks, sorry, gotta take a shower, hey, place looks great, man, did a great job, anybody here yet? I'll be down in five minutes to help you set up, no, Dottie . . ." as he disappeared up the stairs.

Anne gave me a look of equal parts amusement and determination. "Right," she said. "Here's how we'll do it: You get the door; coats and things go in the back closet, let everybody hang their own. Cue music, maybe early Motown to make the mood festive—there's a Temptations greatest hits and a couple of Supremes tapes in my pocketbook."

"Anne, are you by any chance Mary Poppins?"

She smiled. "I'll tell you later. Then I want you to get the ice out of the freezer and into the big tub, *on top of* a case of beer, middle of the table. Seltzer and all the pop on the other end, plastic cups, bag of ice in the green bowl. Then check with me. Got it?"

"Uh-huh." I couldn't actually remember anything that came after "get the door," but I didn't want to disappoint her, and I figured it would come back to me when I wasn't caught in the headlights of her mission-focused eyes.

"Good. I'll go check on the hors d'oeuvres and put out the cookie platters. I'll yell when I need help carrying the punch bowl." She started double-timing it toward the kitchen, then stopped at the bag full of colorfully wrapped lumps. She picked one up and asked, "What's this?"

"Um, it's, uh . . ." I suddenly felt really silly about the whole idea. What was I thinking? "It's party favors. For people's dogs. Homemade dog cookies. Like the ones I make for—"

"What a brilliant idea." She smiled. "No wonder everybody loves you." Just then the doorbell rang and she vanished into the kitchen, her smile still glowing in the space she'd just vacated.

I got to the door just before the canine stampede and opened it as the four dogs came skittering and vocalizing out of the kitchen, Gracie in the lead. I caught her by the collar and gave her my best imitation of Mark declaring "NO!" I must have surprised the other three enough to stop their trajectory toward the door, because they all made the head-jerking-back motion you usually only get to see on sci-fi shows when somebody slams into an invisible force field. "SIT!" I figured I might get them to do something now that I had their attention, but I was clearly pushing my luck—they all shuffled a little and looked back and forth at each other uneasily, and when Merlin (who made Gracie look petite) started undermining my authority, I had a vague fear they were going to burst out laughing.

"WOOF!" he told them in a basso profundo, and for good measure, "WOOF!" I was pretty sure that was his way of saying, *Pay no attention to the two-legged one—he has no legal authority over you.* I was just about to prepare a rebuttal when I heard a very tentative "Hello?" and a "Hi there?" from the guests at the door, whom I'd forgotten. I turned around to greet good old—uh, I-think-I-must-have-met-you-before-but-I-have-no-idea-who-you-are. You know who I mean. They're a lovely couple; I'm sure they've been to your parties, too. And you greeted them with extra enthusiasm, just like I did.

"Oh, *hi!* Come on *in!* Glad you could *make* it! How y'all *do*in'?" I made a big show of ushering them in from the airlock while Sarah, Dottie, Gracie, and Merlin stood around muttering mutinously—or as mutinously as dogs can mutter when each arrival at the door promises an indescribable ecstasy never yet experienced.

"Oh, fine, fine," said the husband. Or boyfriend. Or brother . . .

"Well, *great!*" said the host, thinking, *So you're not gonna help me, are you?* "Here, lemme take your coats and you can go in and make yourselves comfortable."

"Great!" said the . . . female of the two. "Oh, before I for-get," she said, "we brought champagne!" and handed me the bottle with great ceremony.

"Well, actually," said the guy, "it's not champagne, honey, it's sparkling wine."

Honey looked a bit miffed. "What do you mean it's not champagne? What does it look like, Fred—cooking sherry?"

"Well, no, hon, technically only sparkling wines from the Champagne region of France can be called 'champagne,' so even if you use the exact same grapes but grow them in, I don't know, the Rhine Valley, let's say, even if you—"

I was already thinking *Gotta be Mark's friends* when I heard *"Dan!"*

It was Mark to the rescue, shaved and showered and ready to party. "Hey, Anne! Hey, you guys!" As he strode past the dogs a casual "SIT!" pulled the magnets in their butts straight to the floor. He greeted the guests with the energy you can have only if you haven't done any work to make the party happen. "Hey, come on *in!*"

I gave Anne a look.

She gave one back. "Why don't you run upstairs and catch a quick shower and shave? Me and Mark got things pretty well covered down here."

When I returned twenty minutes later the joint was jump-ing—there must have been four or five more dogs and maybe thirty people, most of whom I actually knew (especially the dogs), and all of them looked to be having a good time. I even got a chorus of "Hey, Dan!" that rivaled anything the regulars ever got on *Cheers*. For a second I almost forgot that my life was going nowhere.

I really tried to enjoy the party—I chatted with a bunch of people, drank some beer, ate some of Anne's cookies (normally a foolproof, if short-term, mood elevator). I even danced a little. But around 11:30 I found myself sitting in the kitchen, nursing yet another beer. I wasn't exactly glad to be alone, but it somehow felt less lonely than being in a crowd. Then Anne came in to disturb my reverie.

"Hiding from your adoring fans?"

I turned away and did the not-worth-talking-about-it wave.

"Oh, it is so worth talking about." She pulled up the chair across from me. "You first."

"There's nothing to talk about. I don't know what it is."

"What *what* is?"

I blew out a blast of air. "All right. It's just that . . . I mean, everybody's out there partying, all full of optimism and resolutions for the new year and how things are gonna be different and better, and *they're* gonna be different and better . . . and I'm not."

"No?"

I shook my head. "Just the opposite. I'm thirty years old, in a dead-end job with no prospects of anything better, going seventy-five miles an hour in no particular direction. My whole life I've been thinking things would be better if everything *else* was different—if my family life hadn't been so crazy, if we hadn't been so poor, if anybody had encouraged me, if I'd gone to a better school, if I had a better job or a better boss . . . if only, if only, if only."

"Uh-huh."

"And you know what? None of that stuff is the problem. It's me. *I'm* the reason my life is going nowhere."

Anne raised an eyebrow but didn't stop me.

I went on. "Christmas Day I saw how I'd been blaming all the wrong things. Sitting there with Mark, and his whole family, and the dogs, I realized I'm not lacking anything. I have everything I need to have a good life. The only thing I don't have is the one thing no one else can give me: purpose!" I banged the table. "What am I *doing* with my life?"

Gracie trotted in as if summoned by the vibration and plopped her big head on my thigh. Merlin loped in after her, announcing his arrival with a house-shaking "WOOF!" in case we hadn't noticed him. He took up the same position, balancing his huge boxy head on the tabletop.

I heard Anne take a deep breath, though I wasn't looking at her. "Hey," she said. "I'm going to sound like a kindergarten teacher, but humor me. Sometimes it takes a while for a passion to reveal itself. There's preparation and learning going on that we can't always see while we're waiting."

"But preparation for what? More of the same? This year and next year and the year after? That's *it?*"

I caught her swallowing a smile. "What about your business ideas with Mark?"

I shook my head. "Pipe dreams. We don't know the first thing about business, and what do we think? An idea's gonna just drop down from heaven, into our laps? Come on." I took a swig of beer and banged the bottle on the table.

Anne stood up and came around to where I was sitting. In the living room the artist not yet formerly known as Prince was singing about partying like it was 1999. She put her warm hand on the back of my neck.

"It sounds like you're learning a little about being humble."

"Yeah, sure. Eating humble pie is more like it."

"My mama used to say, a big part of humility is knowing there's more going on—in us, for us, around us—than we'll ever understand. And having faith that God or the universe or whatever you want to call it is taking care of us, leading us where we need to go, and guiding us to the next right thing—if we're paying attention."

For a precious moment I stepped outside my own head and the cramped little universe it lived in and looked at Anne's face. Here was somebody who'd had her own share of hurts and griefs and frustrations—maybe more than her share—telling me that I was being watched over, and guided. I wasn't sure I believed her, but I suddenly felt much better. For no good reason—except that I had opened my heart to a friend, and she had heard me.

I was about to say something to Anne, to let her know that she'd helped, when I felt a familiar human paw on my shoulder and heard, "Hey, you guys—it's three minutes to midnight!" Voice and paw both belonged to Mark.

Anne and I looked up, and Gracie and Merlin stood ready for marching orders, Gracie's tongue dangling sideways out of her mouth. "Dan's feeling a little bit discouraged about his life trajectory."

"Are you kidding me? I never met anybody more poised on the brink of success in my whole life!"

I laughed. "Oh yeah—it's gonna kick in any second now."

"Listen, I know I give you all kinds of grief about some of your crazy ideas, but I had a gut instinct the first time we talked about starting a business that the gods were gonna smile on us, and

I'm telling you I feel it stronger than ever."

I looked at him; he didn't look drunk.

"I'm serious!" he said.

I nodded. "I believe you. I mean, I believe you're serious. I don't know about the gods, though."

"Well, look—they're taking the night off anyway, so let's give 'em a rest. Besides, what about all those great doggy treats? We better give 'em out now 'cause people are gonna start heading home after midnight!"

I shook my head. "Homemade dog biscuits. You don't think that's kind of a stupid thing to give people at a New Year's party?"

Mark said, "Hell, no!"

Anne said, "No way!"

Mark pulled me up out of the chair. "Come on, man. It's a new year, new decade. Who knows what's in store for us?"

The houseful of people counted down to zero then erupted into shouts, cheers, plastic horn blasts, and, of course, a chorus of barks and woofs. Everybody was wishing everybody "Happy New Year!" Someone started singing "Auld Lang Syne" and before long everyone had joined in, smiling and feeling goofy, sad, and good all at the same time.

As we were singing—or barking, as the case may be—I thought about how good it had been for me to tell Anne what was eating me, and what a good friend she was. I turned to Mark, who was trying to outbellow the rest of us, and thought about what a good friend *he* was. And I looked around and found Gracie yowling away, and thought about what a . . . what a perfect Gracie she was. It hit me that this whole holiday had been telling me again and again that I'd been given the gift of friendship. I may not have had clarity, a life plan, or a career path; *but with friends like these,* I thought, *what can't I accomplish?* I couldn't think of a darn thing.

eleven

A Bakery for Dogs?

The phone woke me at the crack of noon on New Year's Day. "Is this Dan?" Voice too bright. Vocal equivalent of sun in window. Need dark. And silence.

Enormous white canine body snuggled up next to me, extremely large, wet snout resting on my shoulder. I snuggled up to the warm, furry form, and thought about how the Eskimos slept with their dogs for warmth. I imagined what that would be like, and then I was in an igloo with the poker-playing dogs from the painting, only we were playing gin rummy, a biscuit a point, country tunes coming out of the radio, and—

"I just had to call and tell you what a great time we had last night, and especially for the doggy biscuits! The boys were *crazy* about them!"

"Mm. Boys?"

"Chester and Lester. *Crazy* about 'em! I just *have* to get that recipe from you, okay? Fred's gone already—he always takes a shift at the hospital on holidays so a resident with kids can have the day off—but he told me to thank you guys for the *great* party. Mark too! Okay, bye!"

I stared at the receiver, fighting my way to consciousness just like hard-boiled private eyes were always doing whenever they got conked on the nut with a sap. I had no idea who just talked to me, and with so much en*thu*siasm! Hold it . . . coming back to me . . . got it—the lovely Mrs. Sparkle, of the Champagne Sparkles. "Ow." Hairy paw on my soft underbelly as Gracie pulled me against her for warmth. I was just drifting back to sleep when I thought *Chester and Lester? They don't really have dogs named— gotta ask Mark about this.*

"Hey, Danny boy. Happy New Year!" Mark was wide awake. "Coffee?" Ah, that was why. He poured me a cup and pushed it across the table. "Phone's been ringing off the hook. We must've gotten seven or eight calls in the last half hour."

"What kind of calls?" My first full sentence of the day—I love coffee.

"From the party. Everybody's calling up and saying thanks for the cookies."

"Oh, that's great." Large gulp. Synapse firing. "Did you say something about the cookies?"

"Yeah, Anne said Merlin scarfed 'em up in about a second, and Tanya said, 'Zoby is totally addicted.' Your sister was a riot, she kept saying, 'You guys should go into business!'"

I looked at Mark and he looked at me. Neither of us said a word. Finally he broke the silence. "Hey, you know my mom said the same thing after she gave her friends the biscuits we made on Christmas."

My mind was spinning a million miles a minute. "Do you think—"

We stopped talking again, both of us halfway out of our seats with the mad-professor look in our eyes.

"She was just kidding, obviously—"

"—Gotta be the stupidest thing I ever heard in my life—"

Both of us shook our heads. I looked over at the girls, who were staring at us. I turned to Gracie. "Well, what do you think?" She cocked her head, smiled, and shrugged her shoulders a fraction of an inch as if to say, *Why not?*

"*They* don't seem to think it's so stupid," Mark said.

We were all mulling the idea over when Mark made the deciding gesture. He pulled a pad, pencil, and calculator out of the kitchen drawer and scribbled something at the top of the page.

There, in block letters, were the words:

"So," he said, getting down to business. "What do you pay for a bag of whole-wheat flour?"

As we sat and brainstormed and added up numbers a strange feeling swept over me, almost like my whole body was smiling. As crackpot as the idea sounded, something about it just felt *right*. I knew it wasn't the kind of million-dollar idea I'd hoped would drop out of heaven into my lap. I didn't even think we'd make any money from it; we'd be lucky to break even. But something about baking natural, fresh, *delicious* treats for dogs struck a chord in me. For starters, it made me think of just how much I love dogs—how much pleasure they give me every day.

The other thing I realized was how much *I liked baking!* That might sound unbelievable given the brief history of my baking career. But each time a batch came out right, I felt intense satisfaction. And each new success made me just a little more daring, a little more creative, a little more willing to experiment. I wasn't exactly ready to go out and buy a chef's hat, but it struck me that I was proud of myself for the first time in a long while.

I tried to imagine what it would be like if Mark and I could make this into a real business. How it would feel to know that all our work, every day, was devoted to improving the lives of the creatures we loved so much—not to mention the lives of the humans they kept around for entertainment. Besides, how hard could starting a bakery be, really?

What I want to write next is, "From that day forward we channeled all our energy into making the dream a reality, and we've never stopped for a second." But the truth reads more like this: From that day forward and for days that turned into weeks, and weeks that turned into months, we fantasized and procrastinated like crazy.

In my defense I must say that fantasy and procrastination are two of my stronger skills; over the years I've honed them from an art to a science and back again. But at the same time, when I look back now I realize that a lot of what we called "spinning our wheels" was a kind of research. For one thing, we became experts on commercial dog food. We visited every local supermarket and pet store to inspect the ingredient labels on every dog food and treat we could find. We decided that being brazen about it was probably better than being sneaky, so we each carried a pad and pencil and walked around like we owned the store. What quickly began to disturb us was the number of *nonfood* ingredients listed on every package we examined—well over half the total, and most of them things we couldn't even pronounce. I had thought we were indulging Sarah and Dottie by feeding them the homemade goodies Gracie truly needed; now I felt guilty about all the years we'd been filling them up with the junk in processed dog food.

"I can understand a preservative if you're storing food in a bomb shelter," Mark said at the table one night, "but when you look at the ingredients, everything you see should be *food*." He leaned over Sarah and Dottie, drill-sergeant style. "Am I right, *laydeez?*"

They barked as if on cue, wagging their tails in furry unison.

"You trained them to do that, didn't you?"

"Hey," he said, palms forward, "the customer is always right."

A month later we learned how right the customer is, and how wrong we could be.

I stayed home one Friday night to catch up on the adventures of those wacky Dukes of Hazzard while plying Gracie with treats. She was lying half asleep with her head in my lap—probably wondering why I wasn't using my free hand to fan her with a palm frond—when Mark burst in and announced:

"The Johnson County Dog Fair. It's only four weeks from tomorrow!"

It wasn't really a dog fair, as it turned out. It was an "event" sponsored by the county mental health society to show people how much their animal companions—(especially dogs)—could do for their psychological well-being (just the kind of thing the pharmaceutical companies don't want you to hear). They were inviting groups and companies to set up tables for a "mere" fifty-dollar donation.

"You think we're ready?" As I spoke Gracie gently removed the biscuit I had in my hand.

"Does that answer your question?" Mark asked, pointing at her. "If the pickiest eater in the canine world loves your biscuits, you're doing something right."

We started in high gear. Night after night plus all day every Saturday and Sunday, for the next four weeks, we baked. Only now we were systematic about it, keeping a log of the various ingredients we tried—carrots, raisins, garlic, granola, apples, cranberries, anything that seemed feasible and healthful for the discerning canine palate. By this time we had already logged hours of investigative phone calls to vet schools around the nation, learning which foods to add to our treats and which to avoid. Originally our test market was only three dogs wide, ranging from the finicky-but-not-impossible Gracie to the if-it-stops-moving-I'll-eat-it Dottie, but word spread through the neighborhood (those dogs just can't keep a secret). By the end of the second week, almost every day brought at least one dog and his human who just happened to be strolling by, wondering what was producing that wonderful aroma. By the third week, we had folks knocking on the door, asking if we had a new batch we wanted to test on their dogs. And we encouraged it—we bought a few dozen brown paper lunch bags and stamped each one with our new rubber stamp, which said KC-K9 and our phone number.

With one week to go before the dog fair, we shifted from high gear into panic. Our goal was to sell a thousand dollars' worth of biscuits at two bucks a pound. There was only one catch: It was logistically impossible.

The first problem was our oven, a Chambers stove that dated back to the 1930s. It could only handle two trays at a time, and each tray held less than two pounds of biscuits. At well over an hour per batch, that meant a minimum of 150 to 175 hours of baking in four weekend days and ten evenings working from 5:30 P.M. to midnight. Nope. No way. Something was gonna have to give, something expendable. Sleep. So for that last week we took turns running an extra cycle each weeknight, one of us staying up until 2 A.M. then walking around like a zombie the next day when it was the other's turn to do the same. Luckily I had Gracie to keep me company on my late shifts—she'd nudge me when I slowed down and dutifully sample each batch.

When the big day came, we were ready. Or so we thought. I drafted my ten-year-old niece Maleah and my twelve-year-old nephew Michael to help us, and they turned out to be the ideal employees: They worked for free, they kept themselves entertained, they kept *us* entertained, and the dogs would do anything they said.

Maleah was an aspiring model, actress, and television journalist; Michael was the kind of good-natured, honest, hardworking kid that most parents only dreamed about—though a bit too literal-minded at times, as I would soon find out.

We had a good table, a colorful sign, a delicious product (especially if you're a dog), friendly smiles, cute kids, fun dogs, and a positive attitude: everything anyone needs to do well at these events. Which is why after an hour we were so baffled: We hadn't sold a single biscuit.

"Okay," I said. "Maybe the pitch is wrong. Michael, do

me a favor. Pretend you're at the fair, you're a dog owner, you see the sign KC-K9 BAKERY—FRESH-BAKED TREATS FOR YOUR DOG! and you're curious."

"Okay. And who are you?"

"I'm me."

"But I don't know you."

"Right."

"Okay." Michael walked a few steps away, then strode up with a jaunty spring in his step. "Hi there!"

"Hi!" I said. "And welcome to KC-K9 Bakery, where we make the best baked treats known to canine-kind."

Michael beamed. "Sounds great!"

Two women carrying a brimming canvas tote bag in each hand were walking toward us. I kept smiling and spoke through my teeth. "Don't just say 'great'—ask me some questions, and then buy a bag."

Michael talked through his own smile. "But Uncle Dan, I only have five dollars to get me through the weekend!"

I could feel my eyes bulging despite my smile. "I'll give it right *back* to you, Michael. It's just for a minute!"

Michael composed himself just as the ladies got to the table. "Well, sir," he said. "I'm sure your biscuits are very good, but I don't see why I should pay two dollars for a bag of them when everyone else is giving things away for free."

"Actually, *our* biscuits are baked—excuse me?"

One of the women chimed in. "The boy's right. You folks are the only ones charging money here. Why should we *buy* your things when everyone else's are free?" She picked up a flyer, scowled at it, and turned to her friend. "Fresh biscuits for dogs. And they want *us* to pay *them!*" The two of them cackled like hens and clucked away.

I turned to my beloved nephew and asked in a polite, clenched voice: "Nobody else is charging anything?"

Michael looked nervous. "Nuh-uh."

"And you *knew* that."

"Uh-huh."

"Didn't you think *we* might want to know?"

Michael's face flushed. "How was *I* supposed to know you didn't know? I thought you were just being greedy!"

"*Greedy!*"

"Look, you guys," Mark cut in, "we'll just have to give the biscuits away and look at it as an investment, okay? So let's all—" Before he could finish we had our next pair of customers, a tall brunette in red sunglasses and her less tall husband sweating under the burden of two shopping bags full of free samples.

She picked up a bag. "Two dollars a bag?"

Michael jumped up. "Two dollars is the regular low price, but today for one day only we're *giving* them away at no cost to you, the consumer! Right, Uncle Dan?"

"Uh, yeah! Yup, that's right—today only, no charge!" I felt like I had just said "Drinks are on me!" in a crowded saloon.

The woman's eyes lit up. "In that case, we'll take five bags!"

I gulped. "Five?"

"Yes, that's one each for Nick and Nora, our Labs, one for Mother's dog Fluffy, and one for Caroline's little dachshund Schnitzel—oh, he is just the cutest little thing!" She paused. "And, you know, one just for emergencies!"

I opened my mouth to say something but never got the chance.

"That's great!" Mark beamed. "Here you go: one, two, three, four, and five. And here's an extra one, for your neighbors and *their* dogs." He was smiling so warmly that all I could do was grab a bag and help them load up.

"Well, listen, guys, we don't want to monopolize your table, so we'll just scurry along, but thank you so much!"

"It's our pleasure," Mark said. "Give us a call when you run out!"

"You bet!" yelled the sweaty spouse, grunting under the weight of the added poundage.

It turned out to be our biggest "sale" of the day. Over the next four hours we stood in the grueling heat while only a couple of dozen people even approached our table. Most looked at our sign, laughed, and kept on walking. It had never occurred to them that dog biscuits could be fresh baked. By the end of the day we'd given away a whopping twenty-three of our five hundred bags.

Around six o'clock, without a word, we loaded everything back onto the truck, dropped the kids off at my sister's, and drove home in silence. That evening we didn't talk about the fair. It was obvious: The business was a bust. When I took Gracie for her walk that night she tugged at her leash playfully and ran around chasing fireflies. She didn't get it at all. I was a failure and she didn't even notice. Or if she noticed, she certainly didn't care.

After Black Saturday, when we couldn't even *give* our biscuits away, nothing less than a sign from God could have raised our spirits. Monday evening we both pulled up from work at the same time and greeted each other with all the enthusiasm of condemned men meeting their executioners.

Even the girls' joy at seeing us didn't pick us up.

As I went into the living room I heard Mark click on the answering machine in the kitchen. There came the muffled tones of a message, then a loud "huh!" I plopped down onto the couch and Gracie sat down next to me. That is, she backed up to the sofa, plopped her rump down, and kept her front legs upright on the floor; all Great Danes do this, but it always makes me smile. Then she slid over so we were hip to hip and sighed. And I sighed. Another message played, and I heard a louder "huh!" from the kitchen. And another message came on.

"Hey, Dan, come here a second."

"What's up?" I yelled.

"C'mere!"

I hoisted myself up from the couch and dragged my tired bones into the kitchen. At least I wouldn't have to bake tonight.

"Yeah?"

Mark was pointing at the answering machine. He had lightning bolts in his eyes. "Listen! Listen!"

". . . how we can get some more, because we're almost all out. So please give us a call at . . ."

Now I was pointing at the machine. "Was that—?"

Mark was practically jumping up and down. "Uh-huh! Uh-huh!"

"They wanted to—?"

"Yup! Yup! Yes they did. Just like the two calls before!"

"Are you serious?"

"Oh yes I am. Oh yes I am!"

By now we were both dancing around the kitchen like a

pair of big-boned Fred Astaires. Sarah and Dottie ran in to join us, all but doing an Irish jig themselves. The machine kept playing—five calls in all, five requests for more. It was only five, but we were in business! Then suddenly I realized something was missing—Gracie. She had gone to sleep on the couch, and the ruckus we were making hadn't disturbed her a bit. Forget the old saw about letting sleeping dogs lie—I rubbed her back, she raised her head and gave me some sugar, and I beckoned her into the kitchen. After all, it wouldn't be a celebration if I didn't dance with my best girl.

It's easy to look back on a time in your life, a day, even a moment, and say, "That's when everything changed." Most of the time we mean a very specific everything—everything in one relationship, in one job, in one project. But for us—me, Mark, Gracie, Dottie, and Sarah—the moment we received those five orders almost everything in all our lives did change. The most immediate difference was our idea of time and how we related to it. Even though we'd spent every free minute in the weeks before the fair baking, it never occurred to us that we might be making that our regular schedule—for the next week, the next month, or the next four years. After that long and frustrating day at the fair, we both assumed we'd crash for a while; that we'd get our lives back.

We didn't. For the next four years we couldn't get a life, *any* life, and once we finally could, there was no getting our old lives back. We may have been dissatisfied with them while we had them, but there's always something bittersweet in looking back at where you were, *who* you were, and knowing you can't go home again.

But that wasn't what I was thinking at the time. I was thinking, *If I can work a little harder, or more efficiently, then we'll get through. Then we'll be all right.*

We had been spending our lunch hours bringing samples to every veterinarian and pet store we could find, and we were making real progress: First we had a half-dozen regular accounts, folks with a standing weekly order; then we had eleven; then twenty-two . . . Accounts picked up, until we had more than we could fill baking twenty-four hours a day in our kitchen. Mark came to the rescue by finding a pizzeria that was going out of business and buying their huge industrial oven on the spot. It wiped out our savings but tripled our output.

A couple of months later we were sitting in the dining room, now our packing and distribution center, going over the accounts. That is, Mark was going over the numbers and I was waiting patiently for him to explain to me how we were doing. I assumed things were getting better, but his brow was knit so tightly I was afraid there was terrible news locked deep in the numbers. Gracie was by my side and we were both leaning forward. The suspense was killing us.

"What *is* it?"

He took a deep breath. "Well, we're in weird position. In one way, we're doing better. We have three times as many standing orders as we had two months ago."

"Great!"

Mark nodded. "It is great, but it's a problem. We can't keep up with them unless we don't sleep."

I thought about the last few weeks. We could never maintain this kind of schedule on an ongoing basis. "Um, is there another option?"

"Yup. One of us quits his job."

I jumped up. "I'll do it! I'll quit my job tomorrow! I'll make the supreme sacrifice!" I couldn't believe it—the day had come!

Mark smirked. "Yeah, always the martyr. Sorry, Saint Dan, but it's not gonna happen."

I sat down. "Why not?"

"Do the math. You make six thousand a year more than I do, *net*. That's five hundred a month more in take-home pay each month. Get it?"

My heart was sinking fast. I got it. If one of us quit his job, it had to be the one with the smaller paycheck. It was official: Our bakery for dogs now had one full-time employee, Mark, and he wasn't getting paid.

As soon as our bakery had to cover the loss of Mark's income *and* all our monthly expenses, we barely broke even. Mark would mix, roll, cut, and bake from 8 A.M. to midnight seven days a week. I would come back from the office around five or six and work till midnight, pulling the same sixteen-hour shifts as Mark on the weekends. The one "break" we had was on Saturday, when we took turns shopping for supplies and making our weekly deliveries. Even with this grueling schedule, there were more months than I can remember when we skipped paying the gas and electric bills so we could pay the mortgage, only to fall behind a month on the mortgage so the utilities wouldn't be cut off.

But the girls remained unfazed. If anything, they were overjoyed to have Mark's round-the-clock attention, and so happy with their new diet that they came dangerously close to being jaded. One Sunday evening Dottie gorged herself to semiconsciousness, then lay down to take a nap next to the table where I was chopping fresh carrots. As I chopped, one of the carrot medallions teetered off the cutting board and kept going, wobbling like a drunken sailor off the edge of the table and landing square on the tip of Dottie's spotted snout. Without opening her eyes, without so much as raising her head off the floor, she tilted her head to one side and let the carrot roll into her mouth. She chewed, swallowed, and kept on sleeping.

But if the girls were in dog-biscuit heaven, we were in dog-biscuit hell. Baking and living in the same place was slowly taking its toll on our sanity, and I came home one day to find Mark and the girls gone. I looked around and saw that someone had etched the following words in the flour that coated the dining room table: LOOKING FOR SPACE. BE BACK SOON.

Mark found a small vacant luncheonette on Thirty-Third Street for three hundred dollars a month. We thanked our lucky dogs and moved in. We had our own bakery, our product was carried in most veterinarians' offices and every pet store in Kansas City, and several new clients signed up with us every month.

Then one Thursday night around ten o'clock, we heard a knock on the bakery door. We exchanged looks. I let Mark answer.

"Hiya, guys. I walk my dog past here every morning around seven, and every night around eleven, and you're always closed. This is the first time I've been home early enough, but I guess you're closed already, huh?" It was an older gentleman in jeans and a sweatshirt, with a beautiful German shepherd–husky mix who had the same sky blue eyes as Gracie. Her name was Sapphire, for the beautiful color. As soon as the girls smelled her, they jumped up from the floor and scrambled over to say hi.

During the canine introductions, Mark looked at me with question marks, and I shrugged back a *Why not?* As usual, improvising brilliantly.

"Uh, yeah, actually, we're technically closed, but come on in!" It was a nice invitation, but a little redundant, since Sapphire had already pulled the man into the store and was in the middle of the mutual sniff-test with Gracie, then Sarah, then Dottie.

He scanned the place, and looked slightly baffled. "Fellas, I don't mean to pry, but where *is* everything?" Since we weren't selling to the public, we didn't have anything to display our wares.

I grabbed a big tray and laid out an assortment of treats. We had expanded our initial biscuit flavor repertoire to include carob chip, oatmeal raisin, toasted coconut almond, honey granola, peanut butter, and the very popular vegetable beef (much tastier than it sounds—I mean, from what I've been told).

I gave Sapphire a sample and she snarfed it right down. Her human companion picked up one of the biscuits and sniffed it. "It's fresh!"

We nodded. "That's the whole idea," Mark said. We told him about our mission to bake the best dog treats in the world. We chatted for a while about how hard it was to find food you'd actually *want* to give your dog, and he bought a two-pound assortment. It was our first retail sale.

Mark closed the door and turned around, grinning.

"Retail," I said, grinning back. I addressed the dogs. "What do you say, girls? Are we ready to go retail?"

Sarah and Dottie wagged their tails in assent, and Gracie wagged in with them a moment later.

If only it had been that easy. First we needed a bakery case. As luck would have it, my brother Tim was doing some remodeling for a supermarket that was throwing one out, and were we interested? *Were* we! Cleaned and fixed up, it looked almost as good as . . . well, it looked pretty good for an old bakery case.

"All we need now," I said, "is a sign everyone can see from

the road so we can catch the commuter traffic and the lunchtime crowd." We put the month's profits into a big sign for the side of the building, visible from the other side of the main road.

That's when we discovered why the luncheonette had gone out of business.

The sign went up on a Saturday. From Monday to Friday I must have called Mark seven or eight times a day.

"Any walk-ins?"

"Not yet."

"Huh. Okay. Call me after the first one."

"Will do."

An hour later: "Any walk-ins yet?"

"Nope. I told you I'd call."

"I know, but it's lunchtime, and I thought maybe you got a big crowd and couldn't call."

"Dan? Dogs don't take lunch."

As it turned out, most folks don't stop for dog food on the way to work—or on the way home from work, either. You've heard the old line about the three most important things in business: "Location, location, location." We had heard it, too, but now we actually understood it.

The one upside of having so few customers was that most of the ones we did have became regulars, and we got to know all of them—and their humans—by name. Gracie made it her job to greet each one of them at the door and walk them to the counter. That was when we started to realize that apart from the treats themselves, Gracie's personality was our biggest asset. And the humans kept telling us the same thing, day after day: "If you guys were in a place with lots of foot traffic, you'd have more business than you'd know what to do with." To which we'd respond: "Sure. Someday."

"Someday" was on somebody's calendar, even if it wasn't on ours. Then on a lovely Sunday morning in April something unprecedented occurred: We caught up on our orders. We had been in business for over two years, without a day off (no kidding—not Christmas, not New Year's, not nothin'!), and for the first time since the fair we had filled every one of our wholesale orders. And since we sold retail only Monday through Saturday . . .

I looked at Mark. "Does this mean we have the rest of the day off?"

He blinked. "I—I think it does!"

"Then let's get *out of here!*"

Without even asking the girls their opinion we piled out of the store, loaded them into the backseat of the truck, and hit the road—for wonderful Weston, Missouri!

I'm willing to believe that Weston, Missouri, is not the first place that comes to your mind when you think getaway, but I'm here to tell you that it should be, oh, at least fifth or sixth on your list—right after Cancún, Paris, Aruba, the Riviera, and Cap d'Antibes, wherever that is. Or maybe it's just a Kansas City thing. It's the town that would have become Kansas City if not for the great flood of '55 (that's 1855!), which rerouted the Missouri River, making the sleepy little backwater village of Possum Trot the place where "everything's up to date" and leaving what was the bustling river town of Weston in the middle of a lot of mud. Most Westoners couldn't be happier about it, though—it's kept the town a picturesque time capsule, quiet and friendly and peaceful during the week, busy and friendly and energetic on the weekends. So that's where we went to get away from our lonely little corner of downtown KC.

We parked the truck and put the girls on leashes, hoping that Weston was a dog-friendly town. We needn't have worried.

Once we were on Main Street we noticed that there were lots of other dogs around, all on leashes and looking pretty happy. Mark and I exchanged a look. We strolled around for a couple of hours, mostly window-shopping—we couldn't have afforded to buy anything even if the girls hadn't been with us—and taking in the warm energy of the scene. Finally we stopped for a break at the Weston Bakery, where we bought a few cookies for ourselves then sat outside, fed the dogs their own treats and people-watched.

"Place like this would be perfect." Mark was doing the spy thing—looking straight ahead and talking very low, almost without moving his lips.

I tried to do the same. "Tell me about it. Rent's probably sky-high, though."

"Maybe. Only one way to find out."

"You mean . . . ?"

"Look," he said pointing down the street. "Look, there's a Realtor."

She was just getting off the phone as we walked in. "I will. Okay. 'Bye now. Hi," she said, noticing us. "What can I do for you—" then, noticing the girls, "—all?"

"Well, we're looking for a retail bakery space," I said. I was trying to show the kind of confident smile you wouldn't see on someone who wanted to open, oh, let's say, a bakery *for dogs!*

The Realtor's jaw dropped—just a little, but enough to notice. "This is kind of funny," she said. "I was just on the phone with the landlord of Weston Bakery, up the street here. Do you know it?"

"Uh, yeah."

"The tenant's moving out on the first of the month. They asked me to keep my eyes and ears open. I told them it might take a while." She smiled a slightly lopsided grin. "Maybe I was wrong."

I was about to burst into song when Mark gave me the *hold-it-a-second* sign. "Do you know what the rent is?"

"It *was* $300, but they'd like to get $325 if they can. That okay?"

Mark and I puffed up like the youngest generation of Rockefellers.

"Absolutely!"

"Not a problem!"

And that's how we got our first retail store.

Now, at this point you might be thinking: "Oh, give me a break—that's an awful lot of coincidences!" I want to assure you personally that every one of the coincidences chronicled here is on record with the Federal Bureau of Coincidences, Blessings, and Miracles. You can check it out yourself, thanks to the Freedom of Coincidental Information Act.

BARK SILENT, BARK DEEP

We had a great first day in the new bakery. Still, for a long time afterward I had knots in my stomach every morning as I drove out. *Will today be as good as that first day, and if it isn't will it mean we've failed, and if we fail . . . ?* Then I'd look at Gracie with her big head out the window, tongue waving, thrilled to be alive and on her way to another day, ready for anything. And my anxiety would start to fade. Once I was working it would disappear completely—until the next morning. I mentioned all these thoughts to Mark one day when Gracie was staring straight into the wind, her big white ears flapping like sheets on the line.

"Of course," he said. "She knows she has everything she needs for a good day: food, friends, and a job to do."

I nodded, almost convinced. "I guess I need to have a little more faith in providence. Or the dog-biscuit fairy."

But Gracie's example didn't really sink in until one summer Sunday morning when a woman came into the Weston store with her son and their Scottish terrier. Mark was in the back with the girls and the goodies, so I greeted them all with a big hello. The mom helloed back, but the boy, who was eight or nine years old, just stared around the store. That's pretty typical—we've noticed over the years that kids can be a little shy, though they usually open up when they meet one of the girls. But something felt different about this boy, and when his mom got his attention by walking over to him and tapping on his shoulder, I realized what it was: He was deaf.

They started signing to each other with a wonderfully animated energy, and I flashed back to a snapshot of me and my best friend David in childhood, sitting on the curb in front of his house, and signing our fool heads off. We must have been about the same age as this little guy. I walked over to them, hoping my ASL hadn't rusted away to dust.

Hi, I signed. *Is this your first time in the store?*

They both looked startled for a second, then started to sign at the same time.

I read about it in the— the mom began.

Where's Gracie? the boy asked, spelling her name.

You know about Gracie?

My mom told me.

It was in the— "Smitty, stay out of there!" She interrupted her signing to keep their Scotty from burying himself in one of the goodie bins. *Sorry about that!*

No problem, I said. *That's why we always bake extra.* I turned to the boy and said, *I'm Dan. What's your name?*

Gary. He looked at his mom. *You said the dogs work in the store!*

Oh, you bet they do, I said. *Right now they're in the back helping my partner Mark with the baking. Would you like to—*

Before I could finish my sentence a certain wet white snout followed by a pair of sky blue eyes popped up under my arm.

Gracie!

She's beautiful, said Gary's mom.

Please, I said. *You'll make her vain.*

Oh, she said, laughing. *Does she understand American Sign Language?*

I told them about our earliest attempts to communicate

with Gracie, and how I'd had to give up on my brilliant idea for American Canine Sign Language and settle for a half-dozen full-body gestures Gracie could understand even from a distance. We were having a good time when I looked down and saw that Gary was sitting on the floor cross-legged, Smitty in his lap and Gracie washing his face with her foot-long tongue. What really got my attention was that Gary was laughing. Out loud. And loudly!

"He doesn't like to talk," Gary's mom said, still signing as she talked. I guessed she did that so he wouldn't think she was trying to leave him out of the conversation, but he wasn't paying us a lick of attention. He was discovering that, with Gracie, attention often comes in the form of licks. "But he likes to sing to dogs, sort of like cooing."

Just as she said that I noticed that Gary had stood halfway up and laid his head on Gracie's neck; he was making a soft "oooo" sound to her while petting her big head. What was strange was that Gracie started making one of her own distinctive sounds, like the lowing of a baritone cow. I wondered if her sound—which she could feel but not hear—was somehow in direct response to Gary's, which he could also feel but not hear.

As you've probably figured out by now, Gracie was not exactly what you'd describe as "aloof." While she wasn't a total affection hound like some canine trollops I could mention (by the way, where *is* Sarah Jean?), she genuinely liked almost everyone she met. She seemed to have radar for the good in people—even people in whom I couldn't see any good at all—and locked right on to it. And she never hesitated to express her good feelings. But something different was going on between her and Gary.

He was oooo-ing, she was mooing, and they were now gazing into each other's eyes with the kind of warmth you usually see between lovers. Gary was stroking Gracie's neck, and she had her head cocked slightly to one side, as if she was listening to his tune while she sang her own, or as if they were harmonizing. It seemed to me that they had a rapport in their shared silence, and a music in the undertones they voiced, that Gracie could never have with me or Mark. But I wasn't jealous. I felt awe, and gratitude, that creatures can speak to each other in voices they can't hear, across a silence that envelops them. Grace makes this possible, I thought.

"Gracie." I almost jumped. It was Gary's mom, standing next to me, watching the same thing. "That's a good name for her." I looked at her wet eyes, and she smiled, a beautiful smile on a face I guessed had seen a few tears.

"Yeah." I nodded, watching Gracie nuzzle Gary's ear.

Gary's mom laughed. "She's telling him a secret."

I smiled and nodded again. What would the secret be? I wondered for a second, then I knew. It was the same secret Gracie had been telling me with every action from the day we met, through the frenzy of the business, the struggle to keep it going, the hard work and the constant worrying—a silent secret that was clear as a bell if only I would listen: *You're complete. You lack nothing. You have everything you need. You are good.*

GRACIE'S ALBUM

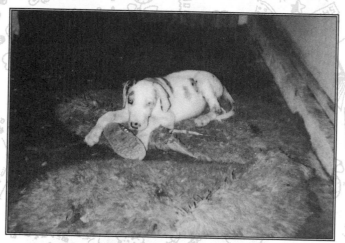

A sad and neglected Gracie as we found her

Gracie's birthday party reveals that
Dottie *(left)* was not the only food thief in the family.

Opening day at the bakery!

 **Employee I.D.**

THE BAKERY FOR DOGS ®

NAME: **Grace Dane**

HIRE DATE: **Day 1**

DEPARTMENT(S): **Quality Control, P.R., General Sniffing**

TASTING CLEARANCE: **All levels**

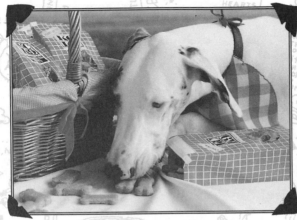

Quality control

Publicity hound—after her appearance on *Oprah*

Two guys, three dogs, and a bakery

Canine Couture: Custom-designed, hand-tailored garments in the finest fabrics can make anyone look . . . dressed up.

BEFORE

AFTER

Gracie and date attend
a Three Dog Bakery
Grand Opening soirée.

Behold, the Great Dane

On the road:
Gracie, Dottie, and Sarah blithely ignore
Sedona's majestic desert landscape and concentrate on dinner.

Three dog day
afternoon at
San Diego's
Dog Beach

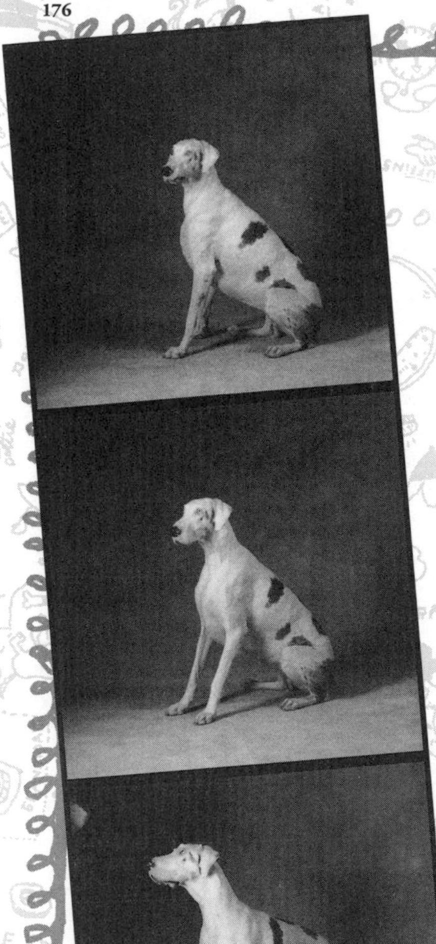

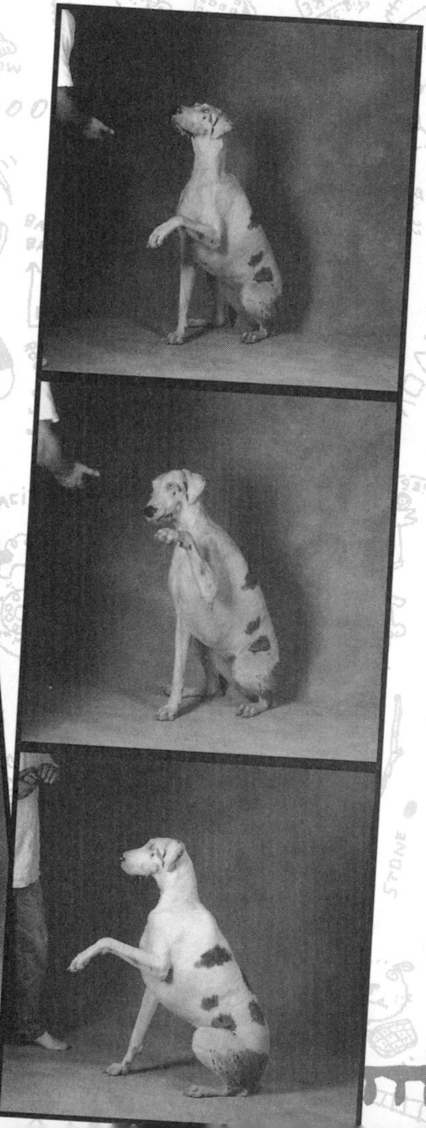

"Okay, fellas.
That's a wrap."

Always obedient

Mama Gracie with her heir, Claire

Goodnight, Gracie.

twelve
Gracie's Prime Time

Some folks don't react well to fame. All that fawning and attention goes to their heads; like babies, they start to think the world revolves around them. That's certainly how *I'd* be if anyone would indulge me long enough.

Not Gracie. Her rise to national renown paralleled the growth of the business she had inspired. All our publicity was free, and most of it came from newspaper people, who loved to take pictures of Gracie and thought the idea of fresh and natural food for dogs was funny. The result was that with Gracie at my side, I could hardly walk down Main Street without being greeted by canines and humans alike. I felt like a celebrity, at least in Kansas City.

Then, toward the end of our fourth year in business, the *Wall Street Journal* published an article about us. Three Dog Bakery shifted into warp drive, and with it Gracie's responsibilities as meeter, greeter, sniffer, and spokesdog (at least to other dogs). Our mail-order business ballooned quickly to ten times its previous size. *Entrepreneur* magazine featured us in an article on unlikely successes, and then—miracle of miracles—Oprah herself invited us onto her show! She held up a dog cookie on national television, sniffed it, considered the ingredients, and then *tasted* it. It was a moment I'll cherish forever: First of all, because only Oprah would have the self-confidence to taste dog cookies in front of an audience of millions without worrying what people might think of her; but more important, because it demonstrated to dog owners everywhere our basic principle of pet food—if it's not fit for us, it's not fit for a dog!

Unfortunately we didn't have enough lead time before our Oprah appearance to bring the dogs with us, so the audience had to meet Gracie, Dottie, and Sarah via satellite. Still, being on the show brought the girls even more attention. Now we were getting written up in magazines and newspapers across the country. All this national exposure meant a lot of interviews, something the girls reacted to very differently. Sarah and Dottie made themselves scarce, either because they suddenly discovered that they were shy (not too likely) or because they didn't want to sully their spotless reputations by contact with "the media" (much more likely). But Gracie seemed to enjoy the attention, and would fix herself to my side the second she saw a microphone pointed in my direction. She would stand perfectly quiet at first, then after about ten minutes she'd give a single throaty, "Woof!" to let the friendly reporter know that we'd had enough: *Okay, folks, one more question, let's wrap it up!* Which is why I was a little nervous when we and the dogs were invited to appear on a particular late-night talk show hosted by a very funny guy on a very large network.

Gracie had been a great publicity hound for us over the years, but she was still a pup when it came to national TV. *Okay,* I thought. *I'm an old hand at this TV thing now, so I can show her the ropes.* I pictured myself telling her and Sarah and Dottie about the etiquette of the green room ("There's lots of food there, and it's very tasty, but try not to eat all of it—oh, and *definitely* don't eat it by sticking your whole face into the bowl. It makes the other guests uncomfortable."), showing them where to place the microphone so it hardly shows ("Under the collar works best for me."), and explaining that pancake makeup—despite its name, look, and aroma—is actually not edible. Then a pretty important question suddenly came to me.

"Mark? How, exactly, are we going to get the girls to New York?"

We had never traveled any farther than the next county with them. We couldn't stand the idea of them cooped up in an airplane's cargo hold for hours, and the back of a pickup truck isn't exactly designed for traveling long distance. Thank goodness for my nephew Michael (by now graduated from high school and working for us full time). He said, "Hey, how about renting a minivan? *Road trip!*"

Road trip it was, though I have to confess that the thought of crossing seven states with a nineteen-year-old nephew, a Mark Beckloff, and almost three hundred pounds of dogs with several tons of personality left me a bit unsettled. I left the logistics to Michael and hoped that God was on our side.

Which He was in the long run (nobody died), but I can't help thinking He had a few laughs at our expense in the short run.

DAY 1 Dottie devoured my wallet, credit cards and all, forcing us to use our petty cash for *all* forms of fuel. Luckily, Michael had emerged from adolescence with a striking resemblance to Prince William, which scored us fast service and gallons of free coffee from cooing young waitresses in roadside diners.

DAY 2 we began to realize just how similar the landscape looks across the country if you're driving on interstates. ("Oh, look. Another McDonald's. Hey, I think this one has *golden* arches!") We also discovered that Sarah must be part bird dog. Why else would she dismember every pillow the motel had seen fit to issue us if not in search of feathers?

DAY 3 Gracie decided that three days of cross-country travel was too much of a good thing. I agreed with her, but only one of us tried to dig a tunnel through the floor of the van. ("Three Dog Bakery Pictures presents . . . William Holden and Grace Dane in . . . *Escape from Stalag Minivan!*") We caught on to her before she actually bored through the metal, but not before she had torn through a blanket and the rubber mat beneath it. While I wasn't overjoyed about Gracie rediscovering her love of excavation just then, I thought we might be able to call on her talents when we got to the Holland Tunnel and encountered a backed-up throng of cars I first mistook for a parking lot.

Mark took this moment to point out that we had ninety minutes to get to the studio. Somehow we'd gotten off schedule and lost a crucial three hours—specifically the three hours during which we would have gotten to the hotel, showered, changed, and put the girls into their designer duds. I had a strong suspicion the delay had something to do with Mark forgetting to arrange the wake-up call that would have gotten us up at 6 A.M. instead of 8:20. I decided not to mention this, or the fact that we might not have woken up even then if Sarah hadn't needed to use the facilities. Thank God for the call of nature.

It took us a mere fifteen minutes to get through the tunnel, and another fifteen minutes to travel two blocks into Manhattan. Michael pointed to our left. "Hey, what's that?" There, in what the map said was the Avenue of the Americas, was what I guessed had to be the largest jam in the recorded history of traffic. Not a good sign.

Mark turned about two degrees in my direction—not much, just enough for me to see his right eyelid twitch. Also not a good sign. Gracie, leaning forward between the bucket seats, shook her huge head and retreated to the back with Dottie and Sarah.

"Wait a second," said Michael. "Let me look at this map . . . Okay, it looks like if we cut across the city going east on Canal, we can go north on Allen Street, which becomes First Avenue, and then take that all the way up to, let's see, odd-numbered streets go west, so 49th Street, and we'll sneak up on Famous Network Studios from behind."

"Michael," I said, blinking. "Are you absolutely sure you've never been to New York?"

He looked startled. "Honest, Uncle Dan—I'm just going by the map!"

Michael proved himself a born navigator and when we pulled up in front of the studio, I stopped waiting to exhale. We were here with eighteen minutes to spare. What else could possibly go wrong?

What's the song say—"if you can make it there, you'll

make it anywhere"? It occurred to me now what this really meant: "*If,* against all odds and despite your best efforts, you *still* somehow make it to New York City . . ." Because no sooner had we gotten into the building and Mark and Sarah and Dottie made it to the elevator banks than Gracie took one look at that black marble floor and decided she was not setting a single paw on it.

Was this really happening? Was my oversized puppy afraid of a shiny marble floor? My mind flashed back to a night a couple of years before, when Gracie had lost her footing going down the basement stairs. The spill was so bad it threw out her right hind knee, and she'd categorically refused to take stairs ever since. What I was seeing right now was the same kind of refusal; *I will not be, I will not be moved.* And for a very simple reason: The floor was as dangerous to her as stairs. It was waxed and polished so shiny bright you could count the whiskers on your snout in the reflection (if you had a snout, and whiskers on it). And that's exactly what was terrifying Gracie. Her long legs and toenails were unable to gain any traction or stability on a floor like that.

Mark yelled, "Hey, stop goofin' around—the elevator's here!"

I looked at him in desperation and yelled back. "She won't walk on the floor!"

Mark smiled at the passersby, who were all staring at us and our canine entourage. Then he turned back to me and said, in a disturbingly calm voice, "Okay. Fine. We now have twelve minutes until the show starts. Why don't you *carry* her?"

A small crowd began to gather, no doubt fascinated by the prospect of seeing a man carry a small horse across the lobby of a midtown Manhattan skyscraper. Never one to turn down a dare, and convinced that the onlookers were prospective fans who must be entertained at all costs, I put Gracie's leash between my teeth and hoisted all 140 pounds of her into the air. Frankly, I don't know which of us was more surprised. As I lumbered toward the elevator, the crowd burst into applause and Mark shook his head.

"Look," he said, "you're famous already."

"Yeah," I grunted. "I hope it's worth the hernia."

Once I had Gracie safely installed in the elevator, Mark got back in behind me with Sarah and Dottie. "You always have to make an entrance, don't you?"

I fixed him with my patented Clint Eastwood stare. "Just be grateful that I'm too mature to mention who forgot to arrange our wake-up call this morning."

Mark stared straight ahead and whistled, observing the international elevator protocol that requires you to pretend everyone else is invisible.

When the doors opened on the sixth floor I was never so happy to see industrial gray carpeting in my life. An associate producer who was waiting for us said our lateness was no problem; we weren't going on the show for a while anyway. So we were over the last hurdle. No more worries. In like Flynn. Though it would have been nice to take a shower . . .

We were in the makeup room, trying to dress the girls while the makeup people did their very best to make us presentable to a national audience (let's just say they don't call them makeup *artists* for nothing). Michael usually helped us get the girls dressed for special occasions, but he was still driving the streets of New York trying to park the van, so we were on our own. I was getting Gracie into her bustle when one of the sound guys came over to fix my battery pack and microphone. I love this technology—the idea that I can have a tiny battery pack on my waist and an even tinier wireless mike on my shirt collar, and all of America can hear me (at least the part that stays up late and watches TV). Unfortunately for all concerned, Gracie shared my fascination with the micro-microphone.

Mr. Audio attached my collar mike and knelt next to my chair while I tightened the chin strap on Gracie's flapper-style hat. The elastic band kept slipping out of its buckle, and when I leaned in to get a closer look, Gracie spotted the mike on my collar. She promptly did what she always did (or tried to do) when faced with an inanimate object that fit into her mouth: She fit it into her mouth. I noticed her jaws snatch at something, but I didn't realize what it was until the audio guy cried out, grabbed the ear of his headset, and fell back on the floor with a Charlie Brown *"aaarrrgghh!"*

I looked at Gracie. She was crunching something. I felt for my collar mike. Gone. "*Gracie!*" That's right—when in panic, yell at the deaf dog. "Gracie, drop it! Drop it!"

Sarah and Dottie started yelling too, one of the other guests ran out yelling "Security!" and Mark dashed over as the sound guy yanked off his headset, moaning. "What's the matter?"

I was trying to pry Gracie's jaws open before she swallowed the microphone, but she wasn't about to give it up—her brow was furrowed with an intensity that said, *Find your own snack!* "She has the mike in her mouth!"

Mark's response? "Drop it, Gracie! Gracie? DROP IT!"

Audio man staggered to his feet. "Now I know what it

sounds like to be eaten by a Great Dane." He looked over at us. "Hey, isn't she the deaf one?"

Mark and I looked at him. "Well, yeah, but—"

He knelt in front of Gracie almost nose to snout, put his hand on her long neck, and let his jaw drop. He stared into her eyes and did it again. She was transfixed—she even stopped chewing. He dropped his jaw one more time, and then stared at the floor and shook his head vigorously. Gracie followed suit, as if we'd been playing Simon Says all afternoon, and the microphone dropped to the floor. Mangled but in one piece.

We thanked the sound guy, his parents, his grandparents, and his kids down to the seventh generation, but he shrugged it off. "Dogs are weird people, man. Gotta talk to 'em in their own language." He turned to me. "I'll get another mike. You might wanna keep it away from Crocodile Rock over here, though." Gracie looked up at us, innocence made flesh.

A security guard stuck his head in the door. "Problem in here?"

Mark and I swapped our own looks of innocence.

"Nope."

"No problem here."

And we believed it, until the assistant producer leaned in past the guard and said, "Three minutes, you guys."

Just then Michael walked in—in time to see Dottie about

to sink her teeth into a container of pancake makeup. He grabbed her before the first chomp.

"You don't want to eat that nasty old makeup. I've got something you *really* want!" Michael produced the rawhide. It was their favorite keep-out-of-trouble snack, and we'd made sure to bring plenty for today, just in case.

We were led out to the wings and I was about to ask if somebody had a newspaper for the girls, when we got the "3—2—1—a-a-and—"

"—Three Dog Bakery, Mark Beckloff and Dan Dye!"

Our appearance was divided into two parts. First we would teach Famous Host how to make Late-Nite Snaps; then, following a commercial break, guys and dogs would meet at Famous's desk to be interviewed. Simple, right? No reason being on television in front of millions of people with three "idiosyncratic" dogs should make us nervous, right?

The first part went pretty well, considering that everything had been laid out for us and we weren't actually cooking so much as demonstrating the preparation and showing the Snaps at various stages in their development. We had to keep the dogs a few feet away to make sure they didn't abscond with the ingredients, and they took no offense—they all had rawhide to conquer. I had to keep reminding myself to breathe, but Famous was so funny that I quickly forgot to be nervous; unfortunately, I also forgot that we weren't sitting at home and watching him on TV. Luckily I had Mark's elbow in my ribs reminding me to *respond* to Famous, and not just laugh at his jokes.

By the time we broke for a commercial, Michael had already brought the dogs over to the regular set. When we took our seats, he gave me a worried look, murmured something like "sorry about the desk," and disappeared into the wings.

I turned to Mark. "What did he say?"

"I don't know. Sounded like 'sorry about the desk' or something."

I looked at Famous's desk, which seemed fine—shinier than I remembered it, but no chomp marks of any kind, unlike our furniture at home. "That's weird," I said. "There's nothing wrong with the—Gracie!" There she was behind the desk, slurping like it was an all-night sucker. The entire top of the desk was covered in what I'll euphemistically call "Gracie lacquer." I grabbed Gracie, pulled her back behind the couch, and gave her the rawhide to chew just as Famous Host was taking his seat, all smiles until Mark whispered, "Sorry about the desk!"

"Why, what's wrong with the—" A split second before his elbows hit the wood, Famous saw exactly what was wrong with the desk. I would have handed him my handkerchief but we were on in "5—4—3—"

It would have been nice if this was the last thing to go

wrong that night. Gracie, God bless her velvety white hide, had other ideas. Or just one, really, but it was a doozy: She decided that, after years of being the lead mascot, the spokesdog, the masthead of Three Dog Bakery, she had stage fright—she categorically refused to come out from behind the couch.

If she'd been smaller, Famous Host might have joked that we didn't even *have* a third dog, but Gracie was just tall enough that you could see her eyes and the top of her snout over the back of the couch, inspiring Famous to do the dum-dum dum-*dum* theme from *Jaws*. If you ever feel compelled to visit New York's Museum of Television and Radio you can dig up that night's show and watch it for yourself (though I sincerely hope you'll have better things to do with your time). You'll notice my left arm hanging behind the couch, trying gently but firmly to nudge Gracie out into the open while cheerfully pretending to be engaged in witty banter with my partner and our charming host as an audience of millions asks, "What's the *matter* with this guy?"

Needless to say, I didn't exactly hold up my end of the conversation, but Mark was as cool as ever, and Famous Host himself never let on that he had come within a heartbeat of ruining a very nice suit. But most important, Gracie managed the feat of appearing on network television in late-night prime time without ever actually being seen.

The next morning the sun was streaking through the hotel

curtains as I lay in bed, savoring my media triumph and consider-ing breakfast possibilities (eggs Benedict . . . eggs Florentine . . . eggs scramblé avec fries . . .) when Gracie started licking my face. The outrage! This face had appeared on late-night national TV—it would surely soon adorn the lunch boxes of teenyboppers—and here she was bathing it in slobber. I'd show her! I'd pretend I didn't even notice. I'd . . .

Right.

I grabbed my Ray-Bans and we headed for the park.

Central Park is, for dogs, what New York City itself is for people: the most numerous and varied collection of creatures in all sizes, colors, breeds, pedigrees, and personalities that you could ever hope to see in close quarters—and most of the time getting along just fine. It was just past seven in the morning, but even on this crisp December Saturday there were already dozens of dogs, with their humans in tow, romping around—and off their leashes. And just as I had imagined, because of Gracie's unmistakable pro-file, people recognized us!

"Hey, how ya doin'?" a big guy with a yellow Lab yelled to us. "Saw ya on Letterman last night!" We waved back. I thought of correcting him, but then I figured it could only improve our reputation if people thought we had been on *both* shows.

"Oh look, it's Gracie!" A tall young woman who could have been a model was talking to her Dalmatian and pointing at us—well, at one of us. "We love you guys!"

"Thanks!" Boy, this celebrity thing felt good!

I let Gracie off the leash near the rest of the dogs. At first she seemed shy and confused, but then she joined the loose pack of pooches romping in the meadow. After about twenty minutes of exploring the glories of nature in the middle of Manhattan, she peeled off from the pack to play with a black standard poodle whose fur was sculpted like topiary art.

From the moment I spotted this Park Avenue pet I thought she was an unlikely match for Gracie, who for all her size looked and acted like a great big kid. Still, if they smelled right to each other, who was I to judge?

Eventually it was time for us to head back to the hotel and get some breakfast, so I tried to get Gracie's attention with the signal Mark and I had painstakingly taught her all those years ago: I threw my arms wide, wiggled my fingers, and waited for her to see me and come back.

She didn't look. I waited. She glanced at me and I wiggled

my fingers really loud. Nothing doing. The poodle was nipping her ears and they had no intention of interrupting their play.

Finally Gracie turned to me full-on from halfway across the park, and I knew this was my big chance. I held my arms wide and wiggled my fingers so hard I thought they were about to fly off my hands. I *knew* she'd come running, the way she always did.

She didn't. She wagged her tail and, I swear, smiled. Then she chased the poodle some more. A small crowd of world-weary New York dog owners had begun to stare at the man in dark sunglasses, flapping his fingers at a dog. I heard someone say, "Isn't that the dog guy from TV?" This fame stuff was *great!*

An elegant blonde emerged from the pack of owners and shouted, it turned out, to the poodle. "Penelope," she cried "come on, sweetie! Time to go!" Penelope turned and trotted toward her, with Gracie bringing up the well-coiffed rear.

"Thanks," I said, nodding to Penelope just as Gracie presented herself. "If you hadn't called her, I'd be chasing after this one."

"Well, they certainly seem to like—" She raised her

sunglasses to look at me and Gracie. "Excuse me." She stared at me again. "This is going to sound stupid, but have you ever heard of Three Dog Bakery?"

I grinned. Who needs privacy when you can have universal recognition? "Yes, I have."

She smiled back and pointed at Gracie. "Is this Gracie?"

"Yes it is." I tried to play it cool—us celebrities like to do that.

Penelope's companion beamed at me. "And you must be Mark!"

I cleared my throat. "Um, actually, I'm Dan."

She blushed. "Oh, I'm so sorry!"

I laughed. It helped that she and her husband had been ordering from us for years, and that they wished we made doggy breakfast, lunch, and dinner. And it didn't hurt that she was an executive for a certain cable television network devoted to eating and cooking and wondered if anyone had approached us about doing a show.

My head was spinning. "Well, not so far . . ."

"Good, 'cause I'm approaching you about it." She pulled out her wallet. "Here's my card. That's my direct line. Can you call Monday morning, say ten-thirty?"

I ♥ NY—where else can you walk your dog on a chilly Saturday morning and come back with an offer for your own TV show? After we parted ways with Penelope and her human I leaned over to Gracie and said, "Don't let me get a swelled head, okay? I know it only lasts for fifteen minutes." Gracie responded by licking the side of my face: *Fame, shmame—where's my breakfast?*

Back at the hotel she ate while I pondered what had just happened in the park. I would have sworn I imagined the whole thing, if not for the fact that two months later we *did* have our own show. If you've ever seen it, you'll recognize me in a heartbeat—I'm the one who's not Mark.

BIG DAY IN SAN DIEGO, PADRE!

But our trip to New York was all prelude to the most glamorous day of Gracie's star-studded career. She was eight years old and we were in San Diego for the simultaneous grand opening of *five* new bakeries! It was the biggest day of our business—though we had already opened a few more locations, we were now doubling our number of stores *in one day*. But this would be as big a day for the girls as it was for us, because we were going to do it in style—doggy-style!

Gracie by now was no stranger to dress-up. Once Mark and I started the business, we pounced on any excuse to costume her and her sisters. It took a while for Sarah and Dottie to develop the patience for it, but Gracie was born for the catwalk—or would have been if not for the unpleasant association with the name. Over the years she graciously submitted to any outfit we concocted. For President's Day she wore a beard and a stovepipe hat (both held to her head with elastic string). For Easter it was a headband with velvety rabbit ears—which looked small compared to her own. For Flag Day she had a Betsy Ross cap and a stars-and-stripes bib. And so on, through Labor Day, Halloween, and Thanksgiving. For our second grand store opening the girls got actual matching dress-and-hat outfits that looked great, although I have to admit they were off the rack (and no, Gracie was never a perfect size six). But this was our first venture into canine couture.

A Kansas City–based clothing designer (for humans—imagine!) had called us up and *asked* if she could custom-make an outfit for each of the girls. We didn't want to be rude, so naturally we accepted her offer of free goods and services. What we didn't know was that she would be making the outfits out of expensive and stunningly beautiful material she had left over from previous works of fashion art—taffeta, organza, tulle, and several other things I wouldn't recognize without House of Style cue cards.

Brenda, the designer, brought the dresses over the day before we were leaving for San Diego. We were stunned—we'd never seen such beautifully made clothing on *people,* let alone dogs.

Sarah's dress was an understated tone-on-tone ruby silk brocade that looked warm and rich next to her black fur and that was set off by a matching headband and huge silk moiré bow. Dottie wore a little crimson paisley number and a jaunty beret, but the best part was the veil on the hat and the matching "train"—naturally, both had polka dots. Yet Gracie's dress and matching pillbox hat somehow outclassed the other two. Made from a royal blue taffeta you'd expect to see on Oscar night, it had so many pleats you could have made four simpler outfits from the same amount of material. The crowning glory of the outfit was the gold lamé that fell like a golden waterfall from the bustle and hat. It was safe to say that there would be no better-dressed dogs at the opening—or anywhere. Throughout space and time.

And don't think our furry *fashionistas* were indifferent to the effect themselves. By now Gracie no longer just submitted to being dolled up, and Sarah and Dottie no longer ran in the opposite direction; over the previous couple of years, for reasons I can't claim to know, every time we brought out a costume of any kind the girls had started to get visibly excited—Gracie most of all! Maybe she liked the extra attention it brought her (not that she lacked for it normally). Maybe she understood that folks put on the swank for special occasions and she wanted to be appropriate. When Brenda unveiled her latest masterpieces Gracie wiggled in a way I hadn't seen her do since she was a puppy. It looked like she was getting tickled from the inside.

Brenda gave each girl a fitting, and with a stitch here and a tuck there the outfits were made perfect, before going back into their boxes to stay safe for the big day.

And now the big day had arrived. Michael was already at the first bakery helping to get things ready when the limousine pulled up in front of our ritzy digs, the Vagabond Motel. Yes, motel. What can I say? The place took dogs, it was conveniently located, and, best of all, it was cheap with a capital CH. From the stunned look on the desk clerk's face I suspect that ours was the first, last, and only stretch limo ever to pull into the Vagabond's lot. It was a gleaming white yacht of a car—a Lincoln Continental on steroids—with dark windows and passenger seats that faced each other across a divide wide enough for a banquet table. Mark and I took the seats that backed up to the driver's, Sarah and Dottie ensconced themselves comfortably at Mark's feet, and Gracie made her stately way to the back sofa. There she took up her favorite sitting position—rump and hind legs on the seat, forepaws on the floor—and gazed out her window, the only one that was slightly opened. For Gracie an open car window had the same therapeutic effect that a back rub has on most humans, but soon she fixed her attention on us. Thus the only thing anyone on the street could see of our party was the noble profile of an enormous dog apparently being chauffeured alone in a stretch limousine, wearing a chic Jackie Kennedy hat. Think of the pomp and circumstance when

Queen Victoria rode in an open carriage for her Jubilee; now imagine her face replaced by Marmaduke's, and you'll get an idea of the effect.

We didn't realize this at first, but we heard so many belly laughs, wolf whistles, and variations on "What in the world . . . ?" that we soon figured it out and had our own belly laughs. Gracie, of course, calmly gazed at us, oblivious to the stir she was creating.

"Look at her," I said. "She doesn't care what anyone says about her." I was feeling smug, and who could blame me?

"You're right," said Mark. "Though it probably helps that she can't *hear* any of it."

Even so. Gracie had the presence and spirit of a Zen master.

And she showed it at the opening. In a celebrity-filled affair that included Morris the Cat and Eddie from *Frazier*, Gracie received hands-down more attention than any of the animals there, including me and Mark, but she never got annoyed or overstimulated. At the first store were two pretty little girls who looked nothing alike but were dressed in matching outfits. They weren't as tall as Gracie, but they fell in love with her—rubbing her fur like it was a big bundle of velvet, playing with her drapery ears, and slipping her dress around her torso so it was completely backward. It wasn't until they tried to ride her like a horsie that she subtly excused herself from their company and came to stand by my side.

There was only one sour note in the whole day, and Gracie managed to make it feel sweet. San Diego has a reputation for being one of the most livable towns, with the most comfortable weather, in the U.S. of A. This gorgeous spring day did nothing to hurt that reputation. Everyone was dressed for a beautiful May afternoon anywhere in the Northern Hemisphere (or November if you live Down Under). That's why we were surprised to see a woman stride into our last store of the day (we'd been trying to spend an hour in each of the stores from one o'clock on) in a full-length mink coat over what might have been riding clothes. She was accompanied not by a dog but by a frazzled-looking young woman whom I took to be her personal assistant. She was not a dog person—she must have seen the grand opening signs and wondered who was bringing down the property values.

"This is ridiculous!" She wasn't proclaiming this to her assistant or even the store in general so much as announcing it to herself. "Gourmet food for dogs? That's the most ridiculous thing I've ever heard in my life!" She turned to the assistant. "Water." The assistant produced water imported from France, where it had been bottled at the source. Of something. Mink Lady took a healthy swig and handed the bottle back without looking for the hand that had given it to her.

I mumbled to Mark, "I can't wait till *I* get that rich and famous."

Mark shook his head. "I can. I can wait a long time."

"And what's *this?*" She had discovered the cake showcase. "Don't tell me these cakes are for dogs!"

"That's it," Mark said under his breath, and made his way to where Madame Mink was holding forth. "Why, yes," he said in his best TV-commercial voice-over style. "These cakes *are* for dogs!" He was turning her rhetorical question into an opportunity. "We bake them fresh daily from all-natural ingredients so every morsel your dog eats is pure nutrition—no additives, preservatives, or artificial flavorings or colorings of any kind." There was an appreciative murmur from the crowd.

"My little Humbert could eat this stuff around the clock," said a tall body-builder type with a beatnik goatee and an adorable mutt at his side.

Madame Mink said, "You have *got* to be kidding."

I couldn't resist the temptation. "We are 100 percent serious! And the proof is in the cake." I turned to Mr. Muscles. "Sir, would you mind volunteering Humbert for a taste test?"

Unfortunately for Humbert, his happy moment had to be postponed. "Oh, I've had enough of this idiocy," said Madame Mink. "We're leaving!"

Now, as soon as we had gotten to this final bakery of the day, Gracie had taken up a position in front of one of the biscuit bins, using the Lucite box as her own personal feedbag. That's where she was during most of this incident. But something must have caught her attention, because the moment Mink Lady announced her departure, Gracie turned around, eyeballed her, walked up behind her, and gave the back of the mink a slimy lick that ran almost from the bottom edge up to between its owner's shoulder blades. The droolly trail her tongue left was studded with biscuit crumbs. Everyone who saw Gracie's work burst out laughing.

"It takes so little to amuse people," she harrumphed— prompting an even bigger wave of laughter.

Humbert's companion started applauding. *"Brava, Gracie! Brava!"* The rest of us picked up the applause, and the bakery was suffused with the particular warmth that happens when strangers are united by a common scorn for snobs. I gave Gracie a great big hug of thanks—for what she'd done, and also for being who she was.

I've thought about Gracie's gesture many times since then, and it always strikes me as deliberate, as if she knew in some uncanny way that this unhappy woman had come into this friendly place to radiate unhappy vibes; she, Gracie, understood instinctively that she had to take swift and effective countermeasures to restore the balance of happiness. Unless of course she just thought Mink Lady was a big furry dog, and she was only trying to give her a lick of hello.

Either way it was a perfect example of her ability to change bad into good so calmly and quietly you could miss it if you blinked.

BEACH BLANKET GRACIE

A half hour later we were ready to leave, but the day was far from over. We were about to reward the girls with a trip to the vacation dream spot of the canine world: San Diego's famous Dog Beach.

When I first heard of Dog Beach, I imagined some dirty plot of sand the size of a backyard on beachfront humans considered unworthy for their own use, covered with garbage and various proofs of the presence of thousands of dogs. Nothing could have been farther from the truth. It was a huge stretch of pristine beach on the bluest water I've ever seen, with a lovely crowd of some of the happiest dogs (and their equally happy owners) you can imagine. There were dogs playing tag, dogs playing Frisbee (no, not with each other—it's Dog *Beach,* not Dog *Heaven*), dogs lolling in the sun, and, most important, dogs romping in the surf. And Gracie was about to go for her first swim.

It's a truism that dogs love to swim—no matter how much

they hate baths. But so many dogs never get the chance to find out. They're never welcome in swimming pools, not everyone lives in easy reach of a beach, and even those who do can have a tough time finding a beach where dogs are allowed on the sand, let alone in the water. So you won't be surprised to hear that, despite the fact that the girls were in the prime of their lives, they had never had a chance to take the plunge. Until today.

We had the stretch limo for the day, so en route to the beach we helped the girls change from formal wear to birthday suits. Then I started rubbing Gracie down with waterproof sunscreen. That's right—albino animals are very sun sensitive, and even nonalbino dogs can get a sunburn. I can only imagine what people thought when a block-long limousine pulled up at the beach, the door opened, and three dogs came flying out, followed by two barefoot guys in cut-offs and T-shirts.

Dottie, the embodiment of acting on instinct, all but took off into orbit the moment we got close enough even to smell the ocean. She bounded over the warm sand and made a running leap into the water. It was still too cold for most humans, but Dottie wasn't interested in ideas like "appropriate temperature"—her mind worked in equations like *big water = swim = NOW!*

Sarah hesitated only a moment before following Dottie. Whatever else she might have been thinking *(Will this ruin my hair?)*, there was no way on earth she would let Dottie have a good time by herself.

Mark, always easily influenced by dogs, went tearing after them—and then tearing right back.

"What's up?"

He shed his T-shirt, shades, and watch. "Hold these, will ya?" He handed them to me and sprinted back to the surf, diving in to play with the rest of the dogs.

Gracie, on the other paw, had to suffer the "Wait up you guys!" torture that youngest kids are always subjected to, and it was my fault. I wasn't finished covering her body with sunscreen yet, and it took another five minutes and the rest of the bottle before I was done (*you* try covering every square inch of a pony's skin with lotion in less than ten minutes!). When she was finally slathered from head to toenails, she scanned the horizon for her sisters and found them faster than I did. She galloped toward them at top speed—but came to a screeching halt at the water's edge.

As she scrutinized the water, her brow furrowed back over the top of her head to the nape of her neck in undulating rolls of white velour. She watched the waves roll onto the beach and danced backward when the water approached her, tiptoeing forward when it receded. She kept looking out to where Sarah and Dottie were splashing in the waves like they'd been doing it all their lives, and then down again at the water in front of her, furrowing her snowy brow even further. She pawed at the water a couple of times, and something surprised her. But what?

Then it hit me: She thought the water was another slippery surface, like a polished floor. But as soon as she figured that she could put her paws *through* the water and down to nice grippable sand, she splashed in up to her knees, then up to her chest, and then—and then she stood there. Statue-esque.

"C'mon Gracie! C'mon, girl!" Mark was beckoning to her from about twenty feet out, where he and Sarah and Dottie were playing catch with a ball someone else had left in the water. Gracie looked back and forth between Mark and me but stayed where she was—she didn't want to come back to me and admit defeat, but she couldn't figure out how to get to Mark and her sisters without getting swallowed up by Big Water. Then, once again, nature came to her aid, this time in the form of a wave that towered over her and plopped on top of her.

I was instantly ready to jump in and rescue my doggy in distress (and possibly win the Boy Scout Medal of Honor), but my heroic impulse went to waste. Gracie's slick head popped up out of the surf; she shook it, looked around, and saw that she was neither touching the ground nor drowning. Then she turned toward Sarah, Dottie, and Mark and did the most natural thing in the world for a dog in water: She dog-paddled. And then she did the most natural thing in the world for her: She stayed and played in the water until everyone else she knew had had enough. After more than an hour of aquatic aerobics she strolled out of the waves and onto the beach like MacArthur returning, came back to our spot, shook herself out all over me, rolled onto the sand, and promptly went to sleep. For me this was a day of Big Business, but for Gracie it was just another day in the sun.

GRACIE TAKES A BITE OUT OF CRIME

We had thought that San Diego was our big adventure for the year, until one November night about six months later when I found myself trying in vain to warm up by the fireplace. I had a cup of hot coffee and my faithful Gracie by my side. Mark was in his usual late-evening position, snoring away on the couch, flanked by two furry bookends. Then suddenly Gracie was standing up and barking.

When Gracie first came to us her senses were not finely honed. She was likely to continue sleeping when we got home from work each day, completely oblivious to Sarah and Dottie barking or dancing around at the door. Often I was able to come into the house and get settled before I went to get her. She always looked embarrassed when I woke her, as if I had caught her slacking off on the job. But as she grew up and reached full doghood, her other senses became extremely keen. If she was sleeping and didn't notice Sarah and Dottie announcing our arrival, she would *smell* us from deep within her slumber. (I attribute this to her powerful nose, and not our pungency; I won't presume to speak for Mark, but for the record *I* use a leading antiperspirant.)

If I was upstairs and Gracie outside, and I wanted her attention, I obviously couldn't just call to her the way I could with Dottie and Sarah (not that they would respond, but at least they could hear me). Usually, I had to locate Gracie in the yard, go downstairs, walk across the porch, cross the yard, and tap her on the behind to get her attention. Sometimes, though, I got to see wondrous examples of her powerful senses. I might be watching her through the kitchen window when all of a sudden her nose would shoot up in the air—high in the air—and she would begin inhaling deeply. Then, like a bolt of lightning, she would streak off to the front yard. Why? She had picked up the scent of the mailman, who might still be several houses away. By the time I got to the front door to confirm my suspicions, the mailman would be at the edge of our sidewalk, usually frozen in place with fear. Gracie may have been deaf, but it was hard to put anything over on her.

Her sense of touch, too, was sharper than a normal dog's. I began to notice that if I made a little thud on the floor with my foot, I could get her attention from across the room. Sarah and Dottie were oblivious to the vibration, but Gracie could feel it—lifting her head, sometimes out of a sound sleep, as if she'd heard something. I used to wonder if she was hearing at a different frequency, or a higher pitch, than other dogs could. On this November night she was proving it. Not a barker by nature, she was bringing up from her insides a ferocious thunder that rattled the house. I couldn't guess what she was barking at, but I knew enough not to try to stop her when she made a dash for the back of the house.

I caught up with her standing with her front paws up on the back door, still barking furiously. I peered out. The dark yard was empty.

"Look," I said. "Nothing." I made the sign for nothing, one hand smoothing out an imaginary table. She kept barking.

Mark appeared with Sarah and Dottie in tow. "What's she barking at?"

"I don't know. She usually saves this for the mailman. But there's nothing there."

I tried to pull her away but she wouldn't budge. I even gave her the signal to *stop*, along with a slight rap on the behind so she'd know I was serious. Nothing doing: There was something she needed in the backyard.

Finally I figured *What the hell* and opened the back door to let her out. She leaped into the darkened yard. Then suddenly the barking stopped.

Mark and I looked at each other. "I'll go out if you do," I said, terrified. I looked up at the ceiling: *Please don't let her be hurt!*

"If you're gonna go out," Mark counteroffered, "why don't I just stay in here?" He cleared his throat. "You know, to guard Dottie and Sarah!"

I shoved him to the back door, though not before he grabbed a baseball bat from the deck. I couldn't see Gracie from the deck, but I knew I'd closed the gates.

"Gra-cie?" I sang out in a whisper.

"Dan?" Mark was about to remind me that she was deaf.

"I know," I said. "What am I supposed to do to get her attention? Stand here in the dark and stink a lot?"

We stepped down to the frozen grass.

"Help," someone was calling in a tiny, breathless voice. "Call your dog offa me."

We moved toward the side of the house near the gate.

Gracie had cornered a man, a burly man in a bulky jacket, against the fence. Her enormous jaw hung wide open and she was growling at a low, steady rumble: "Rrrrrrrrrrrrrrr . . ." As with every true Great Dane, drool was pouring out of her jaw in prodigious quantities—the intruder probably thought she had rabies.

"Will you *please* get your dog outta here?" The large man squeaked out his plea in a voice that said he wasn't quite capable of breathing.

My brain raced to explain why a man dressed in black sweats would be inside our fence at ten o'clock at night. "I'll call 911," I said, heroically retreating to the house. Mark stood there with the Louisville Slugger held high, ready to hit a grand slam in case the burglar tried to bean him with a baseball.

As it turned out, the man was wanted for a long, long string of robberies. He had just broken into the place across the street from us, but was spotted leaving and must have decided that the perfect hiding place was that abandoned wreck of a house—ours.

Big mistake.

Now, normally I'm not the kind of guy to stand up to big, beefy outlaws. Under ordinary circumstances I'm more the suave, sophisticated type. That night, though, waiting for the police to arrive, standing behind my faithful Great Dane and next to my bat-wielding best friend, I felt pretty tough. But we knew who the real hero was.

Gracie, the dog I always felt I had to protect, had stood up in the face of danger and protected us. As the police hauled off the burglar—who seemed grateful to be saved from Gracie's wrath—Mark and I descended on her with hugs and kisses. She looked at us and the corners of her mouth turned up. She may have been famous, but in her heart she knew her most important job was protecting her family—us. She showed her true colors that night—true blue. Autograph hound or no, Gracie was a star to me.

But a star always shines its brightest before it burns out.

thirteen

Motherly Grace

I was talking with Mark about how Gracie was dragging her feet a little more than usual, and how I was worried that the knee she'd popped in her fall down the basement stairs years back was coming back to haunt her. Maybe I needed to take her to visit the chiropractor who'd helped her last year, but—

"Dan, she's getting old."

"Yeah, but she's only nine and—"

"I know. But that's old for a Great Dane."

We were staying late at our new company office—"Three Dog World HQ," as Anne liked to call it. We had had a good meeting with our board, and stuck around to talk with Ron, our CEO and president; he'd left a high-profile position with a Fortune 100 company to help us transform Three Dog Bakery from a local success story to a national chain. Since Ron came on board, we had expanded from eight stores to thirty-two and hired a management dream team whose presence freed me and Mark to do the things that we loved most: visiting our bakeries, handling the company's public relations, focusing on our weekly TV show for the Chow Channel, and best of all, spending more time with dogs. But even Ron had to go home occasionally, and now we were sitting in the boardroom, looking out the wall of windows at Kansas City by night. Dottie and Gracie were asleep, and Sarah was sitting up alert at Mark's ankle, as if she were determined never to miss a decision-making opportunity. It was hard to believe where we were, and how far we had come. But no amount of success was going to protect Gracie from the effects of time.

It was easy to deny it at first. I'd look at Sarah and see all the gray in her whiskers that stood out so starkly against the black of her fur, then I'd look at Gracie and see not a trace of it. Of course I knew that it would be close to impossible to see gray on an albino dog, but it somehow consoled me.

Still, aside from a little trouble standing and sitting, once Gracie was mobile she was perfectly fine—just a little slower. She still greeted everyone she met, still had the same curiosity about the smallest things in the universe, still gave thanks every time she ate, still kept me company everywhere I went. Now that we had real offices, anytime she wasn't actually beside me, I could find her catching a dog-nap under my desk. And when I had to work at the desk myself, we had a favorite position: I'd pull up a chair next to mine, facing me; she'd park her butt on it, still up on her front legs, and deposit her big head square on my lap.

Now I walked over to the warm corner of the boardroom that Gracie had staked out, sat down next to her on the carpet, and stroked her velvety back as she slept. I leaned over her ear and whispered: "Some Great Danes live to twelve or thirteen. Some Great Danes live to twelve or thirteen."

Mark knelt next to me and looked down at her sleeping face. "Hey. She's just getting old, you know—she's not on her way out. She's still got a lotta livin' to do."

I nodded.

"Think of Mrs. McGuire."

That made me smile. Ever since she and Byron had moved to their new home, Mrs. McGuire had sent us a long letter every year at Christmas, telling us how they were doing. Although she needed to use a walker now, she had become the opposite of the recluse she was when we first moved next door to her. A couple of years ago she organized a reading group that met every week and she led the book discussions herself. I imagined her chiding the other members for splitting their infinitives or dangling their modifiers, and I pictured Byron backing her up every step of the way: "Arf!"

"Yeah," I said. "Too bad they don't have assisted living for golden-aged pooches."

"They do," said Mark. "Our place."

Our new house, outside of town, was on twenty-five *fenced-in* acres (the closest thing on earth to doggy heaven) with big insulated windows all around. But the best part was that all but two of the rooms were on one floor. There were *no steps anywhere.*

When we first got the house each dog had systematically set about marking her territory around the property, sniffing every shrub and herb, trotting the perimeter of the fence, and, finally, lying in the sun on the back deck. Basically, country living allowed the girls to do everything God designed dogs to do. The fresh air even seemed to give Gracie more energy to lope around.

I knew country living would be good for the girls, Gracie especially. What I didn't know was how good it would be for me. For the first time in my life as a grown-up, I began to slow down. It was clear that I wouldn't have forever with Gracie, and slowing down gave me more time with her. When the weekend rolled around, if we weren't traveling I actually let myself lounge around and not do a thing. I felt no need to jump in the car and go to a store or a restaurant or a friend's house, let alone the office. I felt a *very* strong desire to stay put. And for the life of me I couldn't think of anything better than to go out on the deck and lie in the sun with Gracie next to me, listening to the breeze and the bees. Or at night to look up at a sky crammed with more stars than I ever guessed the cosmos could hold.

As always, there were other considerations. Like the question of succession.

If the movies are telling the truth (and we have no reason to think they're not), there was a lot of storm and stress about who would succeed Henry VIII to the English throne. Would it be frail young Edward, the male heir Jane Seymour was good enough to give Henry? Would it be Mary, his Catholic daughter by Catherine of Aragon? Or would it be plucky young Bess (Elizabeth to you and me), his Protestant daughter by Anne Boleyn? And what about sweet Jane Grey, Edward's beloved cousin? And that troublemaking Mary, Queen of Scots? The stakes of succession may not have been quite as high for us, but that didn't make it any easier to think about.

It was Ron who first broached the subject—delicately. We were standing in the parking lot one evening.

"Boys, we have to talk about something that I know is gonna be painful. We don't have to talk about it this second, but I wanna put it out there so we all have time to think about it."

I held my breath.

"It's about the girls," Ron continued. "You probably know where I'm going with this."

I didn't, but I was sure I didn't want to.

"I love those three," he said. "I don't think I could love them any more than I do. But—and I know I'm not telling you anything you don't know—they're not getting any younger. And sometime in the near future, we're gonna have to start thinking about whether or not they're going to have . . . successors." Ron let out a breath, like he'd been holding off saying this for a long time.

"I know," said Mark. "I know. I've been thinking about it for a while. I'm sure Dan has, too." He looked at me.

"Oh, yeah." I smiled weakly, having lost the power of speech.

Ron clapped me on the shoulder. "I'm glad. Well, it's nothing that has to be decided today. Just food for thought."

That was putting it mildly. Little as Mark or I wanted to think about it, millions of people across the nation were used to seeing Sarah, Dottie, and Gracie at our grand openings and publicity tours, as well as impromptu visits to the bakeries. People had seen the girls on Oprah, Conan O'Brien, the *Today Show*, CNN, and dozens of others, not to mention our own show. Add to that the photos and print stories that had appeared in hundreds of papers and magazines, and you can understand how some weeks we were getting more than six thousand e-mails and letters! And yes, Mark and I got our share, but I have to admit that the majority were addressed to Sarah, Dottie, and Gracie. On top of that, the girls' images were all over our Web site, our packaging, our company brochures, our labeling, our mail-order Dogalog . . . and did I mention that the company is called Three Dog Bakery? There was no way around it: In the minds of almost everyone who had heard of us, Sarah, Dottie, and Gracie *were* the company.

We picked up the conversation the next day over lunch at our favorite diner (they know to make extra-crispy home fries without our even asking).

"So what are we supposed to do," I asked Mark, "put out a casting call for young Sarah, Dottie, and Gracie look-alikes? Is that what you guys are gonna do if I get hit by a truck? 'Hi, folks! Dan couldn't be with us today, but here's his identical twin cousin, Stan.' Is that the plan?"

Mark got a faraway look, and didn't say anything.

"Well?"

"I'm thinking!" He squinted to prove the point. "I think *Don* would be better."

"Yeah, funny. Oh boy, you're crackin' me up."

"But you know what? Think about it—we have all this space now, acres and acres for a young pup to have adventures in, along with the guidance of three wise canine aunts. We're always telling people how good it is to adopt a rescue dog. Maybe it's time we gave the girls some company."

MY TWO DANES

Because Danes don't live as long, I knew it was logical to think in terms of finding a fitting heir to Gracie's throne first. Logic didn't make it feel better; only Gracie would do that. But I found strength in the thought that we might find a great puppy to carry on in Gracie's pawprints.

"Two requirements," I said. "Has to be a Great Dane, and has to be a rescue—no breeder shopping. And has to be a puppy. That's it."

Mark raised an eyebrow. "That's three requirements."

"You gonna make this easier, or you gonna make this harder?"

As it happened, Mark made it easier. He had the brilliant idea of advertising on our Web site that we were looking for a successor (though God knows never a replacement) for Gracie. We were surprised by the avalanche of e-mails, letters, and postcards addressed to Gracie and wishing her well or thanking her, or addressed to us and empathizing with what we were going through.

A week later Mark was sifting through the three hundred pictures we'd received when he spotted her. Her name was Claire. She was little. She was skinny. She was albino. And she was deaf. Her pictures and story came from the Great Dane Rescue of Houston—they said she had been living with a rough band of homeless people in Beaumont, yet was unbelievably sweet and loving. As a matter of fact, they *warned* us about this: "If you're not *sure* you're interested, you'd better not come down and meet her—if you do, there's no chance you'll leave without her." They also warned us about one other thing: "She thinks the world is her lollipop."

I handed the letter to Mark. He read through it in ten seconds and looked up, something urgent in his eyes. "We have to get this dog!"

Well, he had his heart set on her. Who was I to argue?

As bad timing would have it, we had to tape a segment for our show over the next three days. As good fortune (and character, and breeding) had it, Number One Nephew stepped into the breach. Michael was one of Gracie's best friends, so the minute he heard we needed help he volunteered to pick up Claire.

He came over for dinner that night and spent two hours cuddling with Gracie in front of the fireplace, explaining to her what he was doing and why it wouldn't change their relationship one bit. Gracie responded by wagging her tail and reclining with her head in his lap while he rubbed her belly.

Michael's words echoed my own thoughts. I was excited to meet the newest member of our animal kingdom, but I was also worried that Gracie might think I loved her less. I had nothing to worry about; Gracie still had more to teach me about real love.

Three days later found us all in the driveway, preparing to meet love in the form a twenty-pound furry white rag doll named Claire.

Mark and I were standing by the front door—having left the girls inside—as Michael gingerly set Claire down on the gravel path, pointed to us, and gave her a little pat on the bottom to get her started. Now that we were old hands with deaf dogs, we made big motions to beckon her toward us, and come to us she did—all but crawling, because she had to inspect and *lick* practically every pebble en route.

As Mark snapped pictures, I thought about where she'd come from and what she must have been through. I flashed back to Gracie as a pup, alone and ignored on the cold concrete floor. I couldn't wait any longer; I ran and scooped Claire up.

Mark and Michael and his friends gathered around. They were all talking about the amazing trip, and how they'd managed to cram seventeen hours of driving time each way, each *day*, into sixteen hours including breaks . . . but I was in my own world with Claire, while she slurped up my face. I couldn't believe how small she was. I mean, I've seen thousands and thousands of dogs, plenty of them small dogs, lots of them puppies, but it had been so long since a dog of *mine* was this little.

Mark was grinning. "Forgot they came this size, huh?"

"Yeah, exactly."

"Well, let's enjoy it while we can—as Gracie showed us, it doesn't last very long."

The girls were used to the occasional stray showing up and hanging out until we found him a home, and the occasional sleepover with friends' or family's dogs. Maturity had mellowed them, at least compared to their younger, rowdier days—they didn't go ballistic with excitement at the arrival of a new snout, and they certainly didn't go into red alert the way Sarah and Dottie had over Gracie's arrival. Still, what hadn't changed was their intense curiosity. When I set Claire down in their presence for the first time, they did everything but test her for a top secret security clearance—sniffing every inch of her, poking her little belly with their big snouts, giving her the taste test (kinda makes you grateful dogs aren't doctors), and quizzing her general puppy skills. Happily for all of us, she passed the puppy test. But the girls' scrutiny didn't stop there.

Every time Claire got up to explore her new surroundings, they followed her with their eyes. If she strayed too far, the girls would get up and follow her to see what she was up to. If Claire got too close to anything they considered "property," they would growl or even give her a light nip. I didn't interfere—I wanted Claire to learn on *their* terms what the rules were. And since the pup was barely three months old and generally eager to please, she almost always gave in without a yip of protest. To reinforce the guidelines they were laying down for her, I still respected their pack order—I'd feed Sarah first, then Dottie, Gracie, and, finally, Claire—so that nobody felt threatened or out of place.

But Claire had her own radar, and it homed in on Gracie from the first night. I don't know if she somehow instinctively understood that the two of them were albino, blue eyed, and deaf. She might simply have sensed that Gracie, despite her size, was the biggest pushover of the three. However she figured it out, Gracie was her designated role model, just as Dottie had been Gracie's. And like Gracie, Claire did her best to be Gracie's shadow—following her everywhere, trying to do whatever she did, whenever and however she did it. The only difference was that sometimes Gracie just wanted to nap, and after a few minutes of earnestly imitating napping, Claire would get restless and have to get up and explore. At times I wondered if Claire thought Gracie might even be her mom. Then one day it occurred to me that maybe Gracie thought so too.

The first thing I noticed was that Gracie didn't seem to mind Claire's persistent presence. Maybe it was the family resemblance; maybe it's because Claire was so small (hard to imagine when I look at all 110 pounds of her today). I think she remembered what it was like to be the new pup on the block, and she wanted to make sure Claire had it easier. She certainly put up with things Sarah and Dottie wouldn't have allowed for two seconds.

Sometimes it was *Let's play Attack!* Claire would approach slowly, then suddenly pounce with rump in midair and both front legs stretched out, trying to get Gracie to play. At first Gracie stared down her long nose at the young whippersnapper: *Surely you jest.* But after a day or so she was playing right along, going through the postures of the canine martial arts as if she thought this little doll-size version of herself might actually be a worthy mock-adversary.

Other times it was *Tug-o'-war!* Claire trotted over, her head held high, her fuzzy stuffed snake in her mouth, and she dropped the snake at Gracie's paws like a dare: *Bet you're too scared of me to play Tug-o'-war!* Gracie's eyes would bore down on Claire, then on the snake, and back on Claire: *Can't you find somebody your own size to play with?* But Claire would persist, dragging the fuzzy snake to Gracie each time Gracie turned away, and Gracie would always give in, never letting on for a second that she could fling the snake *and* Claire across the room with a flick of her majestic head.

But their favorite game was one that I would have found terrifying if anybody other than Gracie were involved: *Lion tamer!* Claire would leap up in the air, taking little swats at Gracie's mouth, like she was trying to get something out of it. After a couple of minutes Gracie would open her mighty jaws as if to enclose Claire's entire little head and pantomime biting with the gentlest touch. At that point Claire—whom I thought would be scared to death— would scamper around Gracie two or three times, practically dancing with happiness, before she came back around to "do it again."

Since Gracie had never depended on sound to get attention, she never wasted her time barking at Claire the way Sarah and Dottie did. (*Why is the little one ignoring us? She's as bad as Gracie—always off in her own world!*) When she wanted Claire to stop doing something (for example, rolling in the fireplace ashes), she'd amble over to the scene of the crime, pick Claire up by the scruff, and drag her away. Occasionally she accompanied this with a nip on the rump, which translates as *Now don't forget this!* But once in a while she'd have to show real displeasure. That's when she used the silent snarl.

Claire learned this the first night, when she pushed her luck all the way to the bedroom. We had gotten her a little puppy-size bed, but she wanted to sleep with Gracie. The first time she tried it, Gracie nudged her out with her big snout. The second time, she nipped Claire for a second and then nudged her again. The third time was strike three: Gracie curled her lips back and wrinkled her nose without making a sound—this is how deaf dogs the world over snarl at each other. Claire instinctively understood the silent snarl and backed away, but not far—she shuffled backward, butt-first, and made sad puppy eyes at Gracie's stern expression. After about a minute of locked eyes, Gracie broke. She turned her head the other way, and when Claire timidly shuffled back to Gracie's bed and nestled herself against Gracie's belly, Gracie didn't move. I think she was pretending not to notice the little pipsqueak. But later when Claire curled her round body into a tight little ball and pushed against the big belly in her sleep, Gracie turned toward her and lay still, eyeing her warmly.

Then an incident clinched the mother-daughter bond between Gracie and Claire.

BOOZE HOUND

The saga of Claire's struggle with alcohol began innocently enough. We were having a Halloween party with friends
and family to celebrate Claire's arrival into our home. There were
snacks and beverages galore, including some for the humans. Most
of the guests hadn't met Claire before, and they showered her with
the kissing and cuddling attention she thought her due. The party
was a big success.

The morning after, I valiantly got out of bed despite a
hangover that registered 10 on the Richter scale, and let Claire and
her aunts, Sarah and Dottie, out into the yard. (Gracie decided to
keep me company, in case I needed her help.)

No sooner did I fall back to what Bowery bums call sleep,
than I heard a *thud*. Then another *thud*.

In the depths of my booze-addled soul lurked not an atom
of interest in the source of that noise. I didn't care if it was a grem-
lin hitting the nose of a nuclear warhead with a polo mallet, as long
as I didn't have to wake up. I had dropped back to a labored uncon-
sciousness when I was brought around by a louder THUD. I realized that unless I resigned myself to a series of forty-five-second

naps, I would have to search and destroy the source of the sounds.

I followed them to the back door and looked through the window. Sarah and Dottie were cowering in a corner, watching what I guessed was Claire (I couldn't see from my angle) doing something bad, something they thought could get them *all* in trouble. I heard another THUD as I opened the door.

There, standing before me on the back porch, was Claire, her backside to me, unaware that I was watching her. One of the many places we had stored beer for the party was a gigantic galvanized tub loaded with ice and sitting on the floor of the back deck. As the morning temperature rose, the last remaining beers floated in a cold bath. Claire's face was drenched and dripping with water as she bobbed for beers. When she pinned a can, she'd lift it up out of the tub, then drop it. From the height of her jaws, each drop created a resounding THUD as the beer hit the wooden deck.

Then she would pick the can up, bite through the flimsy aluminum, and lick the beer as it foamed out. I looked out over the backyard—it was littered with her pirate booty, well over a dozen cans, each punctured with her vampire's mark and oozing foamy contents. And Claire? Claire, not to put too fine a point on it, was blitzed. To the gills.

She was starting to stagger when I walked up behind her and gave her a tap on the hip. The tap startled her and she shot off the deck like a bullet, hiding behind the barbecue pit while I cleaned away the remains of the kill and slipped back to my lair; I had my *own* hangover to commune with. But she wasn't abandoned.

Gracie had followed me outside and went over to Claire, gently nudging her wobbly body toward the house. She nudged Claire to her bed and gently curled her enormous body around Claire's little one. She kept watch over Claire this way for the next several hours, forgoing her usual early afternoon outside. When Claire finally woke up, Gracie escorted her to her water dish and then outside. When they came back in, Claire was still a bit green and Gracie once again curled up with her in the bed.

When we'd first gotten Claire, I worried that Gracie might resent the attention I'd be giving the new pup on the block. Seeing the motherly way Gracie doted on Claire now, I wondered if *I* shouldn't be the one to nurse a resentment. The truth was, Gracie seemed as happy when I was paying attention to Claire as when she was. She seemed to know something I was just beginning to learn: that love is not a fixed commodity—and the more you give, the more you have to give.

fourteen

Goodnight, Gracie

After Claire's return to sobriety, she and Gracie were insepara-ble. It wasn't just that she shadowed Gracie everywhere; wherever Gracie went, she was always looking over her shoulder to make sure Claire was close by. It felt like a gift to see the relationship between my two Danes, but a bittersweet one: Gracie's health was beginning to wane.

I noticed that it cost her more effort to lower herself down and pick herself up. Not a ton of effort—just the littlest bit, but that was still a lot more than none. I could actually hear her joints crack-ling when she stood herself up. It was faint at first like someone un-wrapping a hard candy, but if I watched her face I could see that she felt it. Over the course of the past year, the crackling had gotten grad-ually louder.

I had always liked watching Gracie settle down, no matter what she had in mind: scrutinizing a bug or a blade of grass, meditating on her life, watching a movie with me, or turning in for the night. With such long and almost human limbs, she sometimes seemed like a person in a dog suit. At bedtime, though, she was pure dog: She would get into her bed and turn in two or three tight circles while stomping down the cushion (I guess to flatten out any lumps that might have had the nerve to rise up during the day); then, when she had found the exact right position, she'd wiggle her behind, lower herself down, and fall asleep within seconds.

None of this had changed, except for the lowering-down part—as her joints got weaker, she had trouble controlling the pace of the descent. In the past month there really *was* no descent, just a collapsing in place. She would simply drop onto the cushion with a *whomp*. Each time it happened it seemed to startle her, as if she had forgotten what it was like the time before, and the time before that; instead of just dropping off to sleep the way she used to, her blue eyes would pop open and she'd look around like she was trying to find out who had pushed her. Then she'd lie there with her eyes open for a while before letting her guard down and deciding it was okay to sleep.

Aside from her trouble getting up and down, she seemed to be running low on fuel. If we didn't require her attention and Claire couldn't pull her away, Gracie's tendency was to nap. For a few weeks I'd been trying to keep her limber with a slow walk every evening. We would stroll up the gravel driveway, down to the gravel road, meandering at her leisurely pace, Claire literally

running circles around us. Gracie never walked behind or in front
. . . always by my side.

The driveway was over a quarter of a mile long, so the walk
down and back was really a lot of exercise for Gracie. By the time we
got back to the house she was usually panting, ready for a drink of
water and her pillow, but I never once got the sense that she would
rather have stayed home. (Claire, on the other hand, saw the walk
as a warm-up for a marathon she was ready to run *now!*)

But after a month or so, Gracie didn't have the energy even
for driveway strolls. I tried shortening our trip to three-quarters of
the way down the drive; then after a month it was halfway. But by
the time we got back to the house, she would be so winded that I realized she was only doing it for my sake, because she thought I
needed her to walk with me. I started to worry that Claire's high-
speed romps were too exhausting for Gracie, so I left her in the
house and kept this time with Gracie to myself. For the next week,
I cut it back to a quarter of the way down the drive, but I could see
that even this was too much for her—she would lie on the porch
and pant for five minutes, trying to get up enough strength to go
back into the house. So I stopped pushing the walk. Each evening,
as soon as I got back from work, she and I would go and stand on
the porch together, listening to the wind. Or I would listen and
Gracie would point her big nose straight up into the air, reading the
wind. It struck me that I had never done that before, just listened to

the wind. As the nights went on, I realized how much there was to experience—not just the occasional car in the distance, or the animals, or the insects or birds, but the wind itself singing through the leaves and grasses, whispering and tickling our ears.

When I did let Claire join us, she had different ways of relating to Gracie—depending on her mood. Sometimes she would run around and around Gracie's long legs while Gracie stood there like a statue. Other times, the sweetest times, Claire would sidle up to Gracie and point her snout in the air, quietly sniffing the night air with us, content simply to be close to her companion. It's as if she knew that Gracie needed our quiet friendship now more than ever. I was proud to see what a sensitive and caring girl Gracie had raised.

One night toward the end of the year Gracie took a downturn. It was at bedtime, and she went through the same routine as always—the circling, the stomping, the position fixing, the butt wiggling, and then the drop. But this time she miscalculated her position, and her hindquarters slammed onto the hard floor. She let out a gasp, like she'd had the wind knocked out of her, but instead of looking around to find the rascally culprit she fixed her eyes on me.

It was the saddest expression I had ever seen. It was like an admission—to herself as well as to me—of her mortality; that our journey together was coming to an end.

Desperate to do something, I took her to Dr. Franklin, our vet since we'd moved out to the country. He was surprised at how healthy Gracie was internally for a Great Dane her age, but it was clear that something was very wrong, and he promised to call me the next day with the lab results.

When he did, Gracie's message to me was confirmed. Her heart and internal organs were fine, but she had a degenerative nerve disorder spreading throughout her body. As I sat there with the phone in my hand, the vet gently outlined what the next few weeks would be like.

It had been ten years since Gracie first came into my life as a hyperactive teddy bear of a puppy. Now, only a few days since our visit with Dr. Franklin, she could no longer lower her rear end to relieve herself without losing control and falling. We got a special harness to attach around her hind legs and midsection for support, which I would hold up while she used her front legs. Within a week she couldn't even walk without the help of the harness.

Claire became almost physically attached to her at this point—she never left Gracie alone for more than ten minutes at a time. I'd let Claire outside, she'd leap around like she hadn't a care in the world, and then after a few manic minutes she'd bound back to the house and Gracie's side. She may not have understood the medical specifics, but she knew Gracie needed her. I often found her lying in front of Gracie's face, staring at her sadly. A couple of times she brought over the fuzzy snake, but Gracie could barely move, let alone play tug-o'-war. After the second futile try, Claire would lay the snake next to Gracie and moan. It was the sound of heartbreak and it shook me. Claire was losing her mother and I was losing my best friend.

I knew the day was drawing near. I didn't want her to suffer a day too long, but I couldn't stand the thought of saying goodbye a day too early.

"We'll know when the time's right," Mark said. "We'll just know." I saw the pain in his eyes, and I knew that he loved Gracie every bit as much as I did.

I hated having to play God about Gracie's life. It made me want to howl at the moon. Who the hell was I to decide when she should die? I prayed for guidance constantly, even as I held her sling to help her walk. For the next two weeks, I'd come home at lunchtime and race home after work, knowing that now she couldn't even change positions on her pillow on her own. The first thing I'd do was get her in the sling and help her up and outside to do her business. Then we'd hobble back into the house. I'd make sure she lay on the opposite side of her body, to help her circulation and to give her tired old joints a break.

Still, somehow, even though she could no longer stand on her own, when I came home her face brightened to see me. With all her pain, she didn't seem the least bit disoriented or out of touch with reality. It was just that her body was giving out on her.

For the past week we had been bringing Gracie's bowl to her; she'd eat while lying down in her bed. Claire seemed awfully confused about this. She would eat herself—just like Gracie, one kibble at a time—then go watch Gracie, then go back to her own bowl. But she had stopped playing with Gracie now. In fact, it seemed that she had stopped playing altogether.

It was now the second week of January, and Gracie's forelegs were beginning to be affected. Her front paws were starting to curl inward and she was rapidly losing control of them. It was one thing to hoist her enormous body up in the rear with the help of the sling; now that her front end was going it took two of us just to get her up.

Mark would take the front and I'd take the rear, or vice versa. It wasn't just that she was heavy, but that she could no longer move on her own, and I knew she wasn't enjoying it at all. Still, she didn't resist or fight us in any way; she tried her hardest to cooperate and to be a good girl. Then she got worse.

I woke up one morning to find her lying helplessly in her own waste. For the first time, she was losing control of her bodily functions. And I felt the indignity of it all. She was such a proud, fastidious dog. I petted her and cleaned her up and petted her more to let her know that she hadn't done anything wrong and I wasn't angry with her . . . then I saw her eyes. It was the same look of shame I'd seen when she couldn't keep herself from plopping to the ground, but magnified.

As I lay next to her, petting her, oooo-ing in her ear, I felt like two oranges had lodged in my throat. Then my eyes sprang a leak. Then I held my dog, my beautiful, beloved, inspiring, amazing Gracie, and I sobbed. I cried like a little kid. It was time.

I got up, washed my face, called Dr. Franklin, and asked if he could come around 1 P.M. the following day. Preparing to spend the last twenty-four hours of Gracie's life with her, I flew to the supermarket and got the biggest steak I could find—a one-and-a-half-inch-thick sirloin so big it was almost ridiculous. Despite all the trouble we'd had feeding Gracie in her first year and sick as she was now, she hadn't lost her appetite, and I was determined to give her a sumptuous last meal. Claire came in to see what I was doing, and then Sarah and Dottie came in, but none of them tried to get to the food. They seemed to know it was for Gracie, not them. And they didn't seem to mind at all.

As I cooked that steak I thought about all the good times we'd had together. About the adventures and hardships and happiness. I thought about how much she had taught me about faith, compassion, and goodness. As I cooked, tears streamed down my face. Sarah and Dottie sat quietly by me.

Gracie seemed to love her dinner. She ate almost half, which was still a huge amount. I wrapped up the rest in case she wanted it the next day for breakfast. When Mark got back that evening we carried her outside one last time to relieve herself. She and I spent our last evening on the porch smelling the clean, sharp night air.

The next morning could not have been a more appropriate day for saying good-bye. It was gray, drizzly, freezing cold, and it stayed wet and dark all morning long. The household was strangely quiet. There was no TV on, no radio, no music, no barking . . . just small sounds of movement. Sarah and Dottie stayed by Mark as he built a roaring fire in the fireplace, and Claire stayed right next to Gracie as we pulled her bed in front of it.

After her hearty breakfast, we took turns lying down beside her and petting her. Sarah and Dottie kept circling her bed, almost like they were sentries standing guard. Claire lay just a foot or so away, hardly moving at all, with her favorite stuffed snake in her little jaws, just staring at Gracie. Mark and I took turns wandering around the house, barely talking. Gracie was breathing heavy and slow, as if each breath took a separate effort.

I wanted the pain to be over for her; at the same time, I didn't want to say good-bye. I kept looking at the clock. Finally, at five minutes to one, Dr. Franklin's van crunched up the long gravel drive. He pulled to a stop and sat in his van for a moment, mentally preparing himself, I guessed, for what he was about to do.

When he slid open the van's side door and pulled out his black doctor's bag, I felt a wave of gratitude toward him for coming to Gracie's home like this. And then I felt another powerful wave, but this time of anger—and I had the urge to open the door and tell him, *Go away!* It's all a *mistake!*

But it wasn't. The time had come for Gracie to be delivered, to be freed from the worn-out body that was hampering her vibrant spirit. Her dog spirit. She had always carried the weight of the world in her wrinkled Great Dane forehead, always been an old soul who seemed to have come to earth to deliver her own unique brand of magic. She had given everything she had to give. Now it was time for her to leave us.

Mark ushered Sarah, Dottie, and Claire into the kitchen. I don't know what I was thinking, but I went to the stereo and put on a CD of Gregorian chants. Maybe I thought that if these chanting monks filled with air with their ancient sacred songs, God might be nearer to us.

Dr. Franklin walked into the house, nodded to me and Mark, and immediately dropped to his knees beside Gracie's bed. The roaring fire reflected against his skin. Mark and I both put on our strong faces as we knelt beside Gracie, petting her.

He didn't rush things. He talked quietly about Gracie and how much he had enjoyed being her vet. He reminded us what a great dog she was, and what an extraordinary life she had led. Then he gently explained the procedure, stressing that Gracie would feel no pain—she would just drift off to sleep, peacefully.

The sky outside turned a full shade darker. After a few more minutes, with Gracie stretched out, her head cradled in my lap, we were ready. As Dr. Franklin prepared his syringe with the fire hissing and cracking, the monks moved into a dramatic crescendo. Mark and I both had tears streaming down our faces as we watched the needle go in, but Gracie didn't even flinch. She remained still and relaxed as we continued to pet her with all the love in the world in each stroke. And then she was gone.

Dr. Franklin waited a few moments then quietly began putting away his supplies. Mark walked with him to the door and thanked him, then came back to Gracie and continued to pet her, neither of us saying a word.

After a few minutes Mark let Sarah, Dottie, and Claire out of the kitchen to say their good-byes. They immediately approached Gracie's still body and sniffed her. Then Sarah, aloof, regal Sarah, did something extraordinary: She gave each of Gracie's closed eyes a couple of warm, loving licks. Dottie lay down by Gracie's side, her head in her paws. And Claire brought her little stuffed snake over and nudged Gracie's nose once, but only once. When Gracie didn't respond, Claire backed away a few inches and lay down, facing her, and let out a long moan.

I buried my face in Gracie's soft warm fur one last time and whispered. "Goodnight, Gracie."

epilogue
GRACIE

It's been several months now since Gracie died and every day there is at least one hour when the loss feels unbearable to me. I look around at the business we've built, all of us, and marvel at how so much can come from one simple act of love. Sentimental gestures always seemed to me like substitutes for real feeling, but since Gracie passed away I've kept her collar and leash hanging on my bedpost; every night I say a small prayer that I hope reaches to her new home.

I don't think I believe in ghosts anymore, but sometimes I know she's here with me. Oddly enough, I think Claire feels it too. When we sit outside on the porch or by Gracie's grave there is a small stirring in the wind that sounds just like the gentle sound of her steady deep breaths. Sarah and Dottie also keep me busy and seem to understand that I need extra canine attention these days.

The week after Gracie died, Claire crawled into my bed each night or cuddled with me by the fire, trying in her own way, I guessed, to absorb some measure of my grief. I look at Claire every day and marvel at how much and how little like Gracie she is. She has a way with people, putting them at ease and licking everyone that is pure Gracie, but she also has a way of hiding my shoes or chasing butterflies that is all her own.

Just the other day I saw Sarah and Dottie playing with Claire, and even though logically I knew it wasn't Gracie, time slipped for a moment and I was watching Gracie alive again in front of me. Her dog spirit was soaring, her body growing almost visibly, ears flapping over her eyes, tail whipping back and forth like a hydraulic windshield wiper, stumbling over her huge paws as she skidded into the turn to catch up with her sisters. Then stopping on a dime as she saw me, she would cock her head as if to say, *Hey, Dan! Don't you want to come and play?*

When the moment passed, I saw that Sarah and Dottie are much older and slower, but also gentler and more patient—spending their time filling in any gaps Gracie might have left in Claire's education. And I suddenly see myself as well. I'm standing here on my own land, the co-owner of an exciting growing business I love that touches the lives of thousands of people. I'm finally understanding and living the limitless possibilities and joys of my life. Looking across time in this way I realize that I have lost nothing, that I have everything I need, and always have.

So amazing: I used to think I had saved Gracie. But now I realize that all along it was Gracie who was saving me.